GRANDMOMMA'S UNSOLICITED ADVICE

Lyndall Stokes Ridenour

WESTBOW
PRESS®
A DIVISION OF THOMAS NELSON
& ZONDERVAN

Copyright © 2018 Lyndall Stokes Ridenour.

All rights reserved. No part of this book may be used or reproduced by any means, graphic, electronic, or mechanical, including photocopying, recording, taping or by any information storage retrieval system without the written permission of the author except in the case of brief quotations embodied in critical articles and reviews.

WestBow Press books may be ordered through booksellers or by contacting:

WestBow Press
A Division of Thomas Nelson & Zondervan
1663 Liberty Drive
Bloomington, IN 47403
www.westbowpress.com
1 (866) 928-1240

Because of the dynamic nature of the Internet, any web addresses or links contained in this book may have changed since publication and may no longer be valid. The views expressed in this work are solely those of the author and do not necessarily reflect the views of the publisher, and the publisher hereby disclaims any responsibility for them.

Any people depicted in stock imagery provided by Thinkstock are models, and such images are being used for illustrative purposes only. Certain stock imagery © Thinkstock.

ISBN: 978-1-9736-1185-1 (sc)
ISBN: 978-1-9736-1187-5 (hc)
ISBN: 978-1-9736-1186-8 (e)

Library of Congress Control Number: 2017919533

Print information available on the last page.

WestBow Press rev. date: 02/19/2018

Scripture taken from the King James Version of the Bible.

Scripture taken from the American King James Version of the Bible.

Scripture taken from the Webster's Bible Translation of the Bible.

Scripture quoted by permission. Quotations designated (NET©) are from the NET Bible® copyright ©1996-2016 by Biblical Studies Press, L.L.C. http://netbible.com All rights reserved.

Scripture quotations marked HCSB®, are taken from the Holman Christian Standard Bible®, Copyright © 1999, 2000, 2002, 2003, 2009 by Holman Bible Publishers. Used by permission. HCSB® is a federally registered trademark of Holman Bible Publishers.

Scripture quotations are from the ESV® Bible (The Holy Bible, English Standard Version®), copyright © 2001 by Crossway, a publishing ministry of Good News Publishers. Used by permission. All rights reserved.

Scripture taken from the New King James Version®. Copyright © 1982 by Thomas Nelson. Used by permission. All rights reserved.

Scripture quotations are taken from the Holy Bible, New Living Translation, copyright ©1996, 2004, 2007, 2013, 2015 by Tyndale House Foundation. Used by permission of Tyndale House Publishers, Inc., Carol Stream, Illinois 60188. All rights reserved.

The Holy Bible, Berean Study Bible, BSB Copyright ©2016 by Bible Hub. Used by Permission. All Rights Reserved Worldwide.

Scripture quotations marked (NIV) are taken from the Holy Bible, New International Version®, NIV®. Copyright © 1973, 1978, 1984, 2011 by Biblica, Inc.™ Used by permission of Zondervan. All rights reserved worldwide. www.zondervan.com The "NIV" and "New International Version" are trademarks registered in the United States Patent and Trademark Office by Biblica, Inc.™

Scripture quotations taken from the New American Standard Bible® (NASB), Copyright © 1960, 1962, 1963, 1968, 1971, 1972, 1973, 1975, 1977, 1995 by The Lockman Foundation. Used by permission. www.Lockman.org

Scripture taken from the Weymouth New Testament.

GOD'S WORD is a copyrighted work of God's Word to the Nations. Quotations are used by permission. Copyright 1995 by God's Word to the Nations. All rights reserved. New Life Version (NLV) Copyright © 1969 by Christian Literature International.

Scripture taken from the New Heart English Bile.

Lyndall Stokes Ridenour and Roger, her husband of 52 years, are the parents of two, grandparents of nine and great-aunt and great-uncle of five special nieces and nephews. In 2010 Lyndall suffered a dissected aorta and was given a 7% chance of survival. Because of this experience and many other life lessons, her faith has grown stronger and she has felt a peace and hope she wanted to pass on to her loved ones. Lyndall decided to write a book to share with them the importance of having God in their lives. She also wanted them to know what a special book the Bible is and the encouragement she has found in God's word. Lyndall feels blessed to have the opportunity to share her feelings about her love for God and to give Him the glory for all He has done in her life. The book explains "the rest of the story".

Contents

Acknowledgments xi

Introduction xiii
    Letter to Grandchildren xvi
    One More Note from Grandmomma xviii

Dedication xix

Chapter One 1
    Two Boats and a Helicopter..22

Chapter Two 29
    Thoughts about Easter 37
    The Last Statements of Jesus 43
    Where to Find the Story of Easter in the Bible 46

Chapter Three..65

Chapter Four...91
    The Donkey Story..92
    The Ten Commandments (Exodus 20:2-17 NKJV) 107
    Prayer Thoughts.. 110
    The Lord's Prayer 111
    Pope Francis' Five Finger Prayer 113
    17th Century Nun's Prayer 115
    The Serenity Prayer 116

Chapter Five	128
The Twenty-Third Psalm	146
Chapter Six	156
Attitude	162
Chapter Seven	183
Footprints in the Sand	192
The Starfish Story	208
Conclusion	213
My Prayer for You	214

Acknowledgments

This book is definitely not the product of one person. You will read about my special husband and best friend later, but there is no way I would have found the love and support to complete this message without the encouragement of my children (now the parents of their own children). My daughter, Lea Ellen, and her husband, John Agee, and my son, Darren, and his wife, Tina Muldong Ridenour, have encouraged me and listened to my words for all the years I have been working on this book. I don't remember a time when one of them has said, "Oh, Mother. You can't say that!" This is another reason I feel God has guided me throughout all my words. That is not the normal response when I am talking to our grandchildren (especially if I am telling them about their parents). God has truly blessed me with not only loving and caring children to their father and me but also wonderful parents to our grandchildren. They have truly made my life complete, for which I will be forever grateful.

Introduction

As anyone who knows me can attest I never do anything in any regular order. This book is no exception. I have finished all of the book and am now writing the introduction. There is a reason for this. First, I will give a little history of our last ten or so years. My husband, Roger, and I were living in East Tennessee with our family and friends. Our daughter, Lea Ellen, and her husband, John, had blessed us with six wonderful grandchildren (five in six years…whew!) Our son, Darren, and his wife, Tina, had blessed us with three special grandsons to carry on the Ridenour name. We also had special great-nieces and great-nephews, whom we love as if they are our grandchildren. Life was wonderful and never dull. Then, because of the problem with allergies in that area, with that area making the top of every "worst for allergies" list you can find, Roger had several bouts of pneumonia. Each kept getting worse. His doctor told him if he didn't get out of the atmosphere of East Tennessee he might not make it the next time. Thus, our move to Florida. As with so many events in my life, I look back at our time in Florida and realize it was part of God's plan.

In 2010, I suffered a dissected aorta and was given a 7% chance to live, and there was concern I would be a vegetable if I did survive. Because I was in the right place, I had the best medical treatment and am here today to tell about it. That was a terrible time for my family (I slept through a lot of it as I was in a coma for about thirty days). It was during this time Roger started really studying the Bible and decided to summarize it to share with our grandchildren. He is the disciplined one in the family, and he spent several hours each morning studying and writing. It was because of this I started writing to our grandchildren.

Again, if we had not been in Florida I would never have taken time to share in such detail what I want so much for each of them to know. They may someday read it, and that will be so much better than their tuning me out as I talked to them.

I had no plans to make this book available to anyone except my family and close friends. Again, that wasn't God's plan. I put my email address on an advertisement for self-publishing a book so I could get the copies I needed. I received a call from Mr. Eric Schroeder, Senior Publishing Consultant, Westbow Press. After reading my manuscript, Mr. Schroeder offered me an opportunity to make this book public. My first reaction was not to do so, as I am a little insecure about strangers reading my feelings. Then I remembered after my recovery my minister's wife had told me God planned to use me some way. I am now very grateful for the opportunity to share my story and, above all else, give God the Glory.

We are now seeing so many signs leading us back home to Tennessee. We signed the papers yesterday to sell our home in Florida. We are praying Roger's allergies will be okay now. If not, we know God has another plan for us.

Grandchildren

Top to bottom, left to right: Logan, Chase, Sarah Elizabeth, John Patrick, Roger Lee (Trey), Anna Catherine, Matthew, Gracie, Emma Bea and Clark, the dog

I love this picture. Each of you seemed to show his/her individual personality. This was our first Thanksgiving after I had been released from the hospital. What a wonderful day! You are almost seven years older now. How the time flies.

Letter to Grandchildren

I love the Bible. I'm sorry to admit I didn't feel this way when I was your age. I loved God; but to be honest, I found the Bible full of names I couldn't pronounce and things I didn't understand. Memorizing scripture has never come easy for me. I seem to do best when memorizing verses in alphabetical order. Sometimes when I cannot sleep at night, I will go through my verses alphabetically, paying attention to the lessons of each verse. This gives me such a peaceful feeling, and I always go to sleep before I can complete the alphabet. I also find strength and peace while remembering these verses during difficult times in my life. If you do not memorize the verses in this book exactly as written, remember the lessons they teach to encourage you when needed. Poppa is really enjoying writing a summary of the Bible and his opinions for you. You will love it. He has taught me so much and encouraged me to learn even more about God's word. Because of our desire to bring you closer to God, you have given us reason to become even closer ourselves. Thank you!

I first started to write this "book" for you because you are always on my mind and in my prayers. I want so much to give you the encouragement and the answers found in the Bible. This book of my unsolicited advice includes some of my favorite Bible verses and some I just chose because I was determined to find a verse starting with every letter of the alphabet. Needless to say, I didn't even scratch the surface of what can be found in this great book, the Bible. When writing my thoughts about each verse, I realized another wonderful quality of the Bible. You will always find something new every time you read it. Each of these bible verses may have a different meaning for you, depending upon what is happening in your life at the time. After reading my thoughts, think of the verse and see if it will benefit you in something going on in your life. I also have put a little challenge in the book. I have written in one of my messages an explanation to my picture on the author's page of this book. Call me when you find it and I will see who finds it first.

As you know, I have always loved inspirational sayings and stories. I decided to include some of my favorites in my thoughts for the day. Some I heard from my granny and mother. (My dad died when I was nine and my other grandparents died before I was born.) Others I have read in books, on the internet or just made up myself. Just consider it more of Grandmomma's unsolicited advice.

As I was writing this for you, I remembered my mother would always send me devotions she had found which she felt would help me. This was before computers and I still find the original clippings she mailed to me mixed in with my "things to keep". I'm afraid I was not always receptive to her good intentions and her desire to share her strong faith with me. You may feel the same way. What makes so much sense to me and helps me cannot always be shared by my words. Your relationship with God is something no one can give you without your willingness to accept it.

I have no idea how this book will turn out, but I do know I felt so very close to each of you with every word I wrote. That is a wonderful feeling. Poppa and I may not be able to spend as much time with you as we would like, but you are always in our thoughts and prayers. God has blessed us with the best grandchildren anyone could ever dream of having. You have brought so much joy to your Poppa and me. We love each of you very much. As much as we love you, God loves you even more. As you live the wonderful life God has given you, always remember you can do all things through Christ who gives you strength.

One More Note from Grandmomma

It has been almost a year since I wrote my first letter to you, printed the book and gave you a copy. Well, you know I have trouble when it comes to stopping "talking". I missed writing you each morning and decided to start another book. Since even I can only give so much advice, I decided one more chapter would be more than enough. Seven is a special number in the Bible, and making this now a book with seven chapters seemed like a good idea. Biblically speaking, seven is known as a number of completeness and perfection (both physical and spiritual). I cannot promise perfection, but I will promise you Chapter Seven will complete this book and my written advice. I am making no promises about verbal advice. I improvised a little on the letter X, as in all versions of the Bible (using Bible Hub on the computer) I couldn't find a verse that begins with that letter.

I definitely feel God was talking to me as I wrote this book. He knows I need to use my own advice. I also am aware I may be the only one reading this book, but that is okay. This advice is the same for all ages, even if you don't look at it until you find it in a box someday when you are my age. The Bible is ageless and will always be there to offer comfort and guidance for us until we are all reunited face to face with the author.

Again, thank you for letting me share my heart and my life with the greatest grandchildren ever. I love you so much.

Dedication

To Poppa (Roger L. Ridenour)

Your Poppa is truly one of a kind, although several of you have a lot of his traits. This man continues to show me how to enjoy life. It was because of his interest in the Bible and his routine of taking several hours each morning to work on his summary and opinions of the Bible for you that I got the idea for this book. I would write while he was working, and too often would interrupt him to ask his opinion. He has been so helpful to me. We have enjoyed discussing the Bible, as well as talking about all of you. He loves working on his book on a cruise ship, where he has spent many hours writing and proof reading.

Poppa and I celebrated our 52th Anniversary August 28, 2017. He gave me candy for Valentine's Day in the 5th grade, and took me to the 8th Grade, Junior and Senior proms. We went to the same school, same church and I was a cheerleader when he played football and basketball. I went to all of his baseball games, but not as a cheerleader, although I did a lot of cheering. He is my best friend. When people would ask me what I wanted your parents to be when they grew up, I would always answer I wanted them to do something they loved; but most of all, I wanted them to find someone to share their life and be with them through all ups and downs. Life has not always been perfect for us. It never is. Marriage is not a 50/50 contract. Each person has to give 100%. In fact, every relationship works best this way. Sometimes that is easier than other times, but it will always work. Poppa wants to make me happy, and he does. I also try so much to make him happy. Our relationship with God is a bond which has brought us even closer and able to handle whatever life brings our way. We thank God every day for giving us the greatest grandchildren ever, and we pray that you will have a wonderful life with God by your side.

Thank you, Roger, for all of your help and encouragement on this book and on my life. I love you so much.

Chapter One

All Scripture is inspired by God and is useful to teach us what is true and to make us realize what is wrong in our lives. 2 Timothy 3:16 (New Living Translation)

Google did a study in 2010 showing titles to 130 million books that have been published. Of all these books, there is one that stands out as unique. That book is the Bible. Not just the predictions of the birth of Jesus Christ, but also other future events, including those concerning Josiah (1 Kings 13:2) and Cyrus (Isaiah 44:28) by name long before they were born, are proof that this could not be the writings of men without inspiration from God. Many have tried to destroy every copy of the Scriptures, but were unsuccessful. Many books have been written to help with every type of problem you may have, but not one book is complete with every answer needed except the Holy Bible. In this verse, the Apostle Paul is reminding Timothy of his early training in the Holy Scripture and the value of these Scriptures. It is the same for us today. This great book was not written to sit on the coffee table and decorate the room. It was written to show us the way to live on earth and to prepare ourselves for a wonderful life everlasting. The more you read the Bible, the more you love its author.

Today start a new appreciation of your Bible. Make a promise to yourself to take time every day to find something new in the Bible. You will also find sometimes the same verse will have a different meaning each time you read it, depending on what is going on in your life at the time. You can read this great book every day of your life and never stop finding something new. Most of all, you will find a new life that is worth living.

"Be still, and know that I am God! I will be honored by every nation. I will be honored throughout the world." Psalm 46:10 (New Living Translation)

Do you remember the childhood game Freeze? It was hard to stay still. I may be able to keep my body still (Poppa will verify that), but my mind is always going. It is the opinion of many who have written about this verse that 'be still' is God asking us to relax and know that He is God and is in control. God wants us to think and use our mind. He gives us rational thinking and answers to life's problems through His word. The peace that comes when you truly let God into your mind and body is the best feeling ever. Too often I just start talking to God about all my concerns or thanking Him for my list of blessings and don't even think about being still and listening. When I do stop to listen, I find peace in knowing He already knows all of this. It is then I sometimes have a thought that is better than any thought of my own. To me this verse reminds me to quit striving to handle everything myself. I need to trust God and get to know Him better, always aware that nothing can separate me from His love and protection. He is with me always, waiting for me to be aware of His presence.

Today make a conscious effort to be aware of God's presence. Listen. The religious leader Dalai lama had great advice I need to remember. He said, "When you talk, you are only repeating things you already know. When you listen, you may learn something new." Get to know God better. He is truly your best friend ever and will always be by your side. He is definitely a good listener.

"Come, follow Me," Jesus said, "and I will make you fishers of men." Matthew 4:19 (Berean Study Bible)

At the beginning of His preaching, knowing He would eventually leave us, Jesus found disciples to follow Him and become honest witnesses of the truth of things that they had heard and seen. Jesus did not choose the mighty and rich to be His followers. He chose regular people just like you and me. Two such men were common fishermen, Simon Peter and his brother Andrew. Jesus saw them casting nets into the Sea of Galilee. He asked them to follow Him and become fishers of men. Living in Florida on the water, we see a lot of fishing for fish. Lucky for the fish, for as many as are caught, probably millions more are left in the ocean. This is not the same for men/women. The ones "caught" are the lucky ones. Jesus wants all of us to be fishers of men/women. Poppa and I are at an age when many of our friends are dying. In this day and time so many do not attend church, and we worry they might not know Jesus. This makes us even more aware of our need to share our love and belief in Jesus Christ. This is not always easy. Some people are offended, but others take the nibble (as do fish). It is true we can't save everyone we know; but we can pray for them and set an example by our actions and by expressing our love and need for Jesus in our lives.

Today talk to someone about Jesus. It can be someone in your family or a friend. Ask them what they think about Him. Just talk normally as if talking about any interests you have. Start today making it an easy conversation to have. I wish I had started earlier. One of our closest lifetime friends was just killed in an automobile accident and neither Poppa nor I know if he believed in God. I pray that this will never happen again. Please keep "fishing for men" so someday we will all be together forever in Heaven and meet Jesus face to face.

Do not be overcome by evil, but overcome evil with good. Romans 12:21 (English Standard Version)

We all know this verse is true, but most of us instinctively want to do something evil when we feel we have been mistreated. We may feel better for a little while, but there is no doubt repaying evil with evil only makes a bad situation worse and makes it last much longer. Paul tells us how we should treat those who persecute us because of our relationship with Christ. We are taught instead of hating them back, we are to love them as Christ loved us and prayed for us, even while He was suffering on the cross. Paul was forever thankful for the mercy given to him when he met Jesus on the road to Damascus. (Acts 9). Even though Paul had been persecuting Christians, God transformed him, gave him a new life and used him to bring the gospel to the Gentiles. Everyone you meet is fighting a battle you know nothing about. It may be your act of kindness could encourage someone who has been your enemy to become a better person and maybe even a friend. One thing for certain, your kindness will not make you an evil person.

Today do an experiment. If someone does something evil to you, determine if you really want to keep the problem going or do you want to make the situation better? Then react. Remember, repaying evil with evil only causes more evil; whereas if you repay it with good, eventually the evil dies out. Let God use you to show His love to others. Forgiving doesn't mean the damage never existed. It means the damage no longer controls our lives.

Endure hardship as discipline; God is treating you as His children. For what children are not disciplined by their father? Hebrews 12:7 (New International Version)

When this verse was written, children were disciplined by their fathers. Sadly, so many families now have only one parent and the father is not even involved in their lives. Many children lack discipline from anyone. Have you ever had a friend with no discipline from his/her parents? This person is probably a very unhappy person. We all need discipline. I won't say their parents did not love them enough to correct them, but I am so grateful mine did. I really do believe God does not do things just to punish us, but I do believe He causes us to have consequences for our wrong doings to prevent us from repeating these sins. There have been several members of our family who would always (when they were children) get into any mischief they could find. They were always so relieved when they were disciplined and stopped from their wrong doings. Our Heavenly Father will always be with us to show us the way we should live. When we ignore His wishes, He loves us enough to show us consequences for our actions. Next time we will think twice before we do it again.

Today think back to consequences you have experienced because of something you have done wrong. Are you willing to do it again? If the answer is yes, you have a problem. Either you weren't punished enough or you do not care enough. You may need to be more aware of whether you are a true child of God. Do you accept Him as your Heavenly Father and respect Him as the ultimate authority in your life? Don't take His love lightly. You are free to choose, but you are not free from the consequences of your choice.

For from Him and through Him and to Him are all things. To Him be the glory forever. Romans 11:36 (New International Version)

I truly love to say, "To God be the Glory!" Just to say that phrase reminds me of all He has done for all of us. Some people are offended by this expression. When I see an athlete or someone receiving an award give God the glory, I am very appreciative of their attitude. Others see this same speech and think they are just showing off and trying to act like they are a good person. So, what should it matter to anyone? I personally think it is wonderful for someone to give God the glory for anything and everything. Everything comes from God and is controlled by Him. It is by His grace we are given all our blessings, and also by His grace we are given the strength to make it through the trials in our lives. I will forever give God the glory and appreciate all others who do the same.

Today remember this short verse of praise and keep it in your heart. Let it come from your lips during all the good and bad times of your life. Above all else, give God the Glory for all He has done.

Guard your steps as you go to the house of God and draw near to listen rather than to offer the sacrifice of fools; for they do not know they are doing evil. Ecclesiastes 5:1 (New International Version)

Solomon provides excellent instructions regarding the right way to worship God. It was common practice at that time to offer animal sacrifices to God, thinking this would please God and He would forgive their sins. The people did not feel the need to listen to God or to offer words of thanksgiving or "talk" to God in anyway. Because God knew their hearts and knew they were not sincere, He did not accept their sacrifices. We may not offer animal sacrifices today, but it is still tempting to say and do what we think will make God happy and make us look good in His eyes and in the eyes of those watching. God doesn't want long and fancy prayers. He knows when we are sincere. God only wants us to listen to Him and feel His guidance. God wants us to be sincerely sorry for our sins and to strive to live in a way pleasing to Him. How do you enter the House of God? Do you enter ready to worship God?

Today remember God is with you always. Yes, there is a special feeling you get when you enter His house to worship Him; and I highly recommend you find a church where you will have this special experience. However, God is always available to be worshiped and to listen to us. Listen to Him. Seek His guidance and ask for His forgiveness. Then strive to live according to His will. God doesn't want just a religious experience for you. He wants a relationship with you.

He gives strength to the weary and increases the power of the weak. Isaiah 40:29 (New International Version)

This is a very good verse to remember. The problems around us often zap all of our strength, but God is always a source of power. I definitely know this to be true. I am especially glad this is my verse for today. Yesterday I received tests results from my doctor which indicated surgery may be required. Of course, this is not something I wanted to hear. It is scary, but I believe God will be with me and will give me strength to handle whatever comes my way. He has done it so many times before. In fact, with every trial I have had in my life, my faith in God has been made stronger. For this reason, I thank God for giving me these trials. I am thankful for the bad things in life. They have opened my eyes to the good things I wasn't paying attention to before.

Today don't let your problems and worries zap you of your strength. You will find even the strongest people in the world become weak when depending on their own strength. It is only when they ask God, the best strength trainer ever, to show them how to be strong that they renew their strength. No gym nor hard exercise is required. In fact, why carry weight God is already carrying.

Several Days Later:

A test to determine the extent of the aortic valve leakage before surgery was performed. God is good!! The leakage had improved and surgery was no longer necessary.

If anyone has ears to hear, he should listen! Mark 4:23 (New International Version)

Jesus taught many lessons by parables. When He was alone, His disciples and others who were gathered around asked him about the parables. He told them, "You are permitted to understand the secret of the Kingdom of God. But I use parables for everything I say to outsiders so that the Scriptures might be fulfilled: 'When they see what I do, they will learn nothing. When they hear what I say, they will not understand. Otherwise, they will turn to me and be forgiven'. (Isaiah 6:9-10)'" Mark 4:11-12 (New Living Translation). He told them to consider carefully what they heard, as their life would be measured by how they used what they heard. Many of Jesus' parables are recorded in the Bible. They are certainly not always easy to understand, as is the same with most of what is written in the Bible. I have found I understand more when I use the many study guides available in books and on useful websites. This helps me to "listen" carefully and really "hear" what Jesus was teaching. This advice from Jesus is true in all we do. The more we "consider carefully what we hear", not only in the lessons in the Bible but also in the words and needs of all around us, the more we will be given the secret of the kingdom of God and our lives will be measured accordingly.

Today read Mark 4. This chapter contains some of my favorite parables. Do you know what Jesus is teaching in them? If not, find out. If you ask others you may get several opinions. It may be interesting to see how your siblings or friends might interpret these parables. Poppa is giving his interpretations in his book. There are also many websites with information about any verse in the Bible. "Listen and Hear!" We must also" listen and hear" the needs of those around us. "Too often we underestimate the power of a smile, a kind word, a listening ear, an honest compliment, or the smallest act of kindness; all of which can turn someone's life around." Leo Buscaglia

Jesus said, "Do not let your hearts be troubled. Believe in God, believe also in Me. In My Father's house there are many rooms. If it were not so, would I have told you that I go to prepare a place for you? And if I go and prepare a place for you, I will come again and take you to Myself, that where I am you will be also." John 14:1-3 (New International Version)

I want to be ready when Jesus returns to take us to His Father's beautiful house with many rooms. He tells us no one knows when that time will be. I will have to admit the thought of Jesus' second coming is sometimes scary to me. This is definitely not the way I should feel. I think it is the fear of the unknown and life different from how I know it with Poppa and with you. Will I be ready? The Bible plainly states we should not let our hearts be troubled. Why do we ever feel apprehensive? Jesus is preparing a place for us. How exciting it will be to meet Jesus face to face. Jesus spoke these words when He knew the end of His life on earth was growing near. He let us know He was leaving His Spirit with us to give us guidance and help us be prepared for His return.

Today think about how Jesus would judge your actions. It is true you cannot work your way to heaven by good deeds. You just need to accept Jesus as your Lord and Savior. When you do this, you will want to live by His example. Are you? We all slip up and make mistakes. Jesus understands and died on the cross so we could be forgiven. Try not to make the same mistake over and over. You will find Jesus' example is the way to have a wonderful life on earth and always be ready for the day when He takes us to His beautiful home in Paradise.

Keep your servant from deliberate sins! Don't let them control me. Then I will be free of guilt and innocent of great sin. Psalm 19:13 (New Living Translation)

The psalmist, King David, was aware he needed God's help to keep him from deliberate sins that had a bad influence on his life and probably the life of others around him. Some sins may have more serious consequences than others; however, a sin is a sin. This verse made me aware of one my deliberate sins of not using my time wisely. Too often I choose to waste time playing solitaire on the computer or watching television, knowing I could be using that time helping others or doing something useful. It isn't a sin to be on the computer or even watch decent television, but everything should be done in moderation. The subject of moderation brings up more of my willful sins. I eat too much and exercise too little. It is a sin, I feel, not to take care of the body God has given me. I know this but continue to ignore it. These may seem like small sins; however, I know my life would be better if I didn't let these "sins" control me. What controls your life? Not too many people try to influence you to sin when you are as old as I am. However, you still have many years of new experiences and new people and influences in your life.

Today notice what you wish you had done differently or had not done at all. What do you deliberately do even though you know your life would be more pleasing to God if you avoided it? Guilt is not always a bad feeling. Let that feeling guide you to a guilt-free and more productive and peaceful life. Do not let anyone or anything other than God gain control over your actions. Remember, everything you do throughout your life is based on the choices you make. You and only you are responsible for your decisions and your actions. As Poppa always says, "Use your head."

Let all bitterness, and wrath, and anger, and clamour, and evil speaking, be put away from you, with all malice. Ephesians 4:31 (King James Bible)

Paul wrote these words to the people of the church in Ephesus encouraging them not to live any longer like other people in the world. He reminded them their purpose is to prepare God's people to serve and to build up the body of Christ. He said they should be patient with each other and lovingly accept each other, no longer being influenced by people using clever strategies to lead them astray. This is also very good advice for us today. When studying this verse, it was amazing how many verses throughout the Bible give this same advice. Out of all the examples of bitterness, rage, etc. given, not one time is there anything other than a bad result. Can you think of any time you have had these emotions and felt any peace or happiness? On the other hand, how many times has your kindness been contagious, causing peace and happiness in you and those around you? "People who fly into a rage always make a bad landing." (Will Rogers)

Today check your attitude. Are you quick to see the bad in a situation? Stop to determine if it really is that bad before you react. When you are mad at someone you love, be careful what you say. Your anger will eventually leave, but you cannot take back your words. When you are bitter and angry it affects everyone around you. Do you want them bitter also? Does that make you happy? Believe it or not, it does make some people happy to see others upset. Be careful you are not one of those people. Try looking for good in the events of the day. Is your cup half full or half empty? I truly hope it is half full so you can enjoy a wonderful cup of life and share that cup of happiness with others.

May the Lord keep watch between you and me even though we are away from each other. Genesis 31:49 (New International Version)

I found this verse in one of my Bible Bingo moments. (Bible Bingo is when you open the Bible randomly and choose a verse on that page… not really the best way to read the Bible.) I read this while Poppa was in Haiti on a mission trip with our church. You will find in using the Bible randomly, the real purpose of the verse in the Bible may have nothing to do with how you see it. Some people will pick a verse in the Bible to prove a point that may not be the message intended when it was written. I agree this is wrong. However, I don't think God would object to using a verse to give you comfort in a situation in your life. This prayer was between Jacob and his father-in-law, Laban, when Jacob had left in secrecy with Laban's daughters and grandchildren. When I read this verse, it was especially meaningful to me for a different reason. I was missing Poppa. Even though I was very happy for him and proud of his desire to go on this mission trip, we are very seldom separated and I was lost without him. This scripture gave me such peace to know the Lord was watching over both of us even though we were apart. I also remember this verse when we are away from you and your parents. It is so wonderful to know God is with all of us everywhere and at all times.

Today be aware of God's presence in your life. As you become older there will be times when you will be separated from your loved ones for different reasons. Isn't it a good feeling to know when we are away from our loved ones God is always there for each of us?

No temptation has overtaken you that is not common to man. God is faithful, and he will not let you be tempted beyond your ability, but with the temptation he will also provide the way of escape, that you may be able to endure it. 1 Corinthians 10:13 (English Standard Version)

I would love to think none of you would give into all the temptations before you today. When Poppa and I were your age the biggest temptations we had in school were to maybe cheat on a test or play hooky (skip school). The class before us had several who did drink alcohol; and the class after us had the same problem, plus two girls got pregnant and had to drop out of school. Luckily, our class was not into any of that. Oh, for the good old days for you. Please remember God gives you a way to escape all these temptations that may seem so important now but can literally ruin your life. Be careful with the computer. You will find it is easier to give into temptation because when writing you are not having to face someone and react. You will write and plan things on the internet you might not in person. Too many behaviors are accepted in society today; however, even though accepted, the consequences are still the same. This subject is not something you want to hear from your grandmother, but please know I have seen a lot of lives ruined by the temptations of the young. What seems like fun becomes a destructive addiction. Also, what seems like a romantic love becomes a very hurtful and destructive relationship. Seek God's guidance in all your life's decisions. Don't rush into something you will regret your entire life. Remember the verse above. Nothing tempting you is new to man, but God will direct you into a way to know what is right and give you an out to what should be avoided. He has also given you very caring parents to guide you.

Today do not write or do anything you would not want seen by anyone, especially your Heavenly Father.

Only a fool despises a parent's discipline; whoever learns from correction is wise. **Proverbs 15:5 (New Living Translation)**

The Lord appeared to King Solomon in a dream and told him to ask for anything he wanted God to give him. Solomon was now king in the place of his father, David, and he was lacking confidence to carry out the duties of a king. He asked God to give him an understanding heart so he could govern God's people well and know the difference between right and wrong. (1 King 3). God granted Solomon's request and gave him even more because he was unselfish in his request. Much of Solomon's wisdom is written in the Book of Proverbs. We too can gain wisdom from reading Solomon's words. Today's verse is one that touches every person's life. We all have parents or people of authority who correct us when we do wrong. There have been many times in my life when I have resented being told what to do. However, there have also been many times when I was glad I followed instructions. Too often when I did not obey I suffered the unpleasant consequences. It is true we learn from our mistakes, but it is also good to be blessed with parents who love us and have already made some of the mistakes they see us making. We should listen and learn by their experiences. Believe me, you will still make mistakes. Then you will want to protect your children from making the same ones.

Today pay attention when your parents correct you. Do you agree you should do as they say, although you would rather not? Sometimes we react the same way to God. We know what we should do but choose to ignore His will. Remember, no one loves you more than your God and your parents (and grandparents). God does not make mistakes, and your parents are right more often than they are not when disciplining you. Learn from your corrections. Be wise.

....Providing for honest things, not only in the sight of the Lord, but also in the sight of men. 2 Corinthians 8:21 (King James Bible)

In this chapter Paul is writing to the Church in Corinth regarding the financial support they have been given. He is warning them to avoid any criticism of the way they administer this generous gift. He explained when they have once lost their reputation, their ministry becomes useless. Paul knew how much his own usefulness depended on his unquestionable character. We should follow the example of Paul. Nothing is easier than to criticize a follower of Christ, and nothing pleases a wicked world more than to be able to do so. God has given each of us a generous gift of His grace and love. How will we use this gift? Certainly, not to the same extent as Paul, but we too have the opportunity to spread the gospel. We should always be aware if we are setting an example pleasing to God and to those watching us. It is amazing to me how many times someone has told me something I said or did which I didn't even remember. Luckily, they were good things. What is sad is that people seem to remember the bad things you do more than the good. Reputations made in early school years stay with you for a long time, sometimes forever. We are given the opportunity to affect the lives of others with every breath we take. Always be aware of your actions, striving to be pleasing in the sight of God and in the sight of others.

Today think before you act or speak. Will you be pleasing God and encouraging others around you to live as you do? Let the difficult people in your life show you who you do not want to be. At the end of the day reflect on your day. Do you have any regrets? Isn't it wonderful God forgives and gives us another chance? People are not that easy. They remember and are less forgiving. I certainly prefer God's way. How about you?

....'Quick! Bring the best robe and put it on him. Put a ring on his finger and sandals on his feet. Bring the fattened calf and kill it. Let's have a feast and celebrate. For this son of mine was dead and is alive again; he was lost and is found.' So they began to celebrate. **Luke 15:22-24 (New International Version)**

Do you remember the parable of the Prodigal Son? This has been a hard parable for me to understand and accept. Jesus did not make His parables easy. He wanted us to search for the meaning. I found my interpretation depended on where I was in my life. As a wife, I saw Poppa as the son who was always there, and I somewhat resented his parents getting so excited when his brother came to visit. As a mother, I understood the joy felt when a child who seemed to have lost his/her way returns home. Sometimes life doesn't seem fair. Maybe you have always tried to do what is pleasing and find your behavior seems to be taken for granted, while someone else has been a discipline problem and is praised when he/she behaves. You may be assured your parents are very proud and appreciative of your good behavior. The truth is, we are not supposed to do what is right to receive praise but because that is God's will for our lives. God loves and accepts all loyal believers into His kingdom. However, He is especially joyful when a sinner turns to Him. Jesus said, "There will be more rejoicing in heaven over one sinner who repents than over ninety-nine righteous persons who do not need to repent" (for they already will receive their reward in Heaven). Luke 15:7 (NIV). As the father of the prodigal son told the older brother, "You are always with me, and everything I have is yours. But we had to celebrate and be glad, because this brother of yours was dead and is alive again; he was lost and is found." Luke 14:31-32 (NIV)

Today read the parable of the Prodigal Son in Luke 15. Put yourself in the place of the father. Would you be excited if your lost son came home? Would you still love the son who remained with you as much as you always have? This is how God rejoices when any sinner finds his way back to Him. What a celebration!!!

Repent, then, and turn to God, so that your sins may be wiped out, that times of refreshing may come from the Lord. Acts 3:19 (New International Version)

When I first read this verse I only interpreted it to mean our sins will be forgiven. When I think of my sins, I think of times I have done something obviously wrong in the eyes of God. When I read it again, I thought about all of the "times of refreshing" I have had in my life. Often these times have come after I have committed the sin of omission by leaving God out of my life, usually when things were going so well and I didn't feel the need for His help. That is why I have often thanked God for my problems. It was then I returned to Him and realized how much I needed Him in my life. God has never left me; however, I have allowed other things to get in the way of my relationship with Him. I am so grateful He has always forgiven me and welcomed me back into His loving arms. This is why I strive to take time each day to go to God in prayer and thank Him for always loving me and giving me a fresh start every day of my life.

Today think about yesterday. Did God even enter your mind? Make an effort today to accept God as a part of your life. You don't need Wi Fi to stay connected to God. He is always available and He is free!

See additional thoughts on the next page.

Additional Thoughts for Previous Page

Poppa and I just returned from a ten-day cruise. This time we did get Wi Fi for the entire trip and were able to keep in touch with family and friends......not free. While we were on this trip we enjoyed the entertainment of a very talented group of young people. The lyrics to one of their songs really touched my heart. Part of these lyrics are: "I'm starting with the man in the mirror. I'm asking him to change his ways. No message could have been any clearer. If you want to make the world a better place, take a look at yourself and then make the change. You gotta get it right while you got the time." Now on days when I feel discouraged because I can't do as much as I once could and feel I am holding Poppa back, I remember I need to "look at the man (woman) in the mirror" and make the world a better place for Poppa and for me by starting with myself to change my attitude and begin to smile. I need to be aware of my many blessings and the fact that I am able to do as much as I do. The lyrics to the rest of this song mentions all of the people with real problems.... those without homes or even food and the list goes on and on. Yes, our world is filled with so many problems and so much sadness. It is true we cannot fix it alone, but we certainly can fix ourselves by starting each day looking at the person in the mirror and asking him/her to make life better for all with whom we come in contact. The woman in my mirror may not be as young and wrinkle free as she once was, but she is definitely a blessed woman whose "sins have been wiped out that times of refreshing may come from the Lord." What we really need to do each day is to take a look into our heart and invite God to guide us to make this world a better place. I may not be able to do as much as I once could, but I am still able to help others, even if only by changing my attitude. It is wonderful to know that you are never too old or too sick to remember others in your prayers. One of my favorite songs gives the best advice for the whole world, "Let there be peace on earth, and let it begin with me".

Start children off on the way they should go, and even when they are old they will not turn from it. Proverbs 22:6 (New International Version)

I remember reading this verse when my children were younger and hoping and praying this was true. I am sure my mother prayed the same prayer for my siblings and me. The older I have gotten, the more I realize how true this verse is. It was because of the examples set by a Christian mother and the training I was given by being taken to church and taught God's word as a young child that I now am aware of God's love and comfort in all I do. It is because of the peace I have found by having a relationship with God that I am writing this book. I want to share my life lessons with my grandchildren, hoping they will learn to always turn to God and find this same peace which cannot be explained. It is also my prayer they will pass on their faith when I am blessed with great-grandchildren (no hurry). We all may stray, but we will not stray far when we remember our Christian teachings. Isn't it wonderful it doesn't really matter how far we stray, God will rejoice when we return to Him, forgive us, and give us a new life in His Son, Jesus Christ.

Today have a talk with God. Yes, He already knows your thoughts and problems; but you will be surprised how it helps to tell Him about them anyway. Just be aware He is always with you. Now make an effort to always be with Him.

"The kingdom of heaven is like a mustard seed, which a man took and planted in his field. Though it is the smallest of all seeds, yet when it grows, it is the largest of garden plants and becomes a tree, so that the birds come and perch in its branches." Matthew 13:31-32 (New International Version)

The Lord answered, "If you had faith even as small as a mustard seed, you could say to this mulberry tree, 'May you be uprooted and thrown into the sea,' and it would obey you! Luke 17:6 (New Living Translation)

I chose these Bible verses because I have always loved the parable of the mustard seed and the examples Jesus used in His teachings. I will have to admit, I am not sure if I could uproot a tree and throw it into the sea; although one time I did jump a wall and lift a lawnmower off Poppa. I know God gave me the strength because there was no way I could have done that on my own. Just this last week I saw a miracle I feel was an answer to faith in God. Test results showed my leaky aorta valve had progressed enough that serious open-heart surgery might be needed. When doing one more test to see what would be involved in the surgery, my cardiologist found the leakage was not as bad as originally thought and surgery was no longer necessary. I know God did it, in spite of my doubt it would happen. I asked God for healing; but because He had answered so many of my prayers for health problems in our family before this latest episode, I really felt I was asking too much of Him. I did have faith God would take care of me, one way or another; but He showed me I needed to have more faith in my prayers. This book would be more than you would want to read if I wrote all the many times I have seen God's work in my life and in the life of others with faith the size of a mustard seed.

Today do not be afraid to ask God for miracles. He may not answer just exactly the way you may want; but know His answer will come in His own time and will be the answer you need. While you are waiting for the answer, be aware of what is happening in your life and the choices God is providing. Have patience and remember it does take time for the mustard seed to become a tree.

Two Boats and a Helicopter

I have heard the story of a man, who was a firm believer of God. One day it began to rain very heavily. It kept raining and a big flood came. The man climbed up on the roof of his house, and knew that he would be ok. God would protect him. It kept raining until the water reached his waist. A boat came by and a guy in the boat told the man to jump in and go with him. "No thanks", said the man. "I'm a firm believer in God. He will rescue me". He sent the boat away. It kept on raining and now the water had reached his neck. Another boat came by and a guy in the boat said: "You look like you could need some help. Jump in and we will take you with us". The man gave the same answer and that boat sailed away. It still rained and the water now reached his mouth. A helicopter came by and a guy in the helicopter threw down a rope and said: "Hi there my friend. Climb up. We will rescue you". "No", said the man. "I'm a firm believer in God. He will rescue me. I know he will". The helicopter flew away. It kept on raining, and finally the man drowned. When the man died, he went to heaven. When entering Heaven, he had an interview with God. After giving a polite greeting and sitting down, the man asked: "Where were you. I waited and waited. I was sure you would rescue me, as I have been a firm believer all my life, and have only done good to others. So where were you when I needed you?" God scratched his confused looking face and answered: "I don't get it either. I sent you two boats and a helicopter".

Many who believe in God somehow believes that signs of help and guidance come as a big event of some kind, when actually it would probably come as small signs of help here and there along the way. Listen to the world around you. You might just find the answer there.

Understanding is a fountain of life to one who has it, but the discipline of fools is folly. Proverbs 16:22 (New American Standard Bible)

Often Jesus used parables difficult to understand in His teachings. In one of His sermons he told the crowd, "To those who listen to my teaching, more understanding will be given. But for those who are not listening, even what little understanding they have will be taken away from them." (Mark 4:25 NLT) This is great advice for us to remember in all we do. I know the more I have read the Bible and have strived to understand the meanings, the better my quality of life has become. In years past when I only did a hit and miss in my Bible study, my life was lacking the peace felt when understanding God's presence in my life. This search for understanding will also be important in every phase of your life. The more you strive to understand your teachers, the better your education will be. The more education you receive, the more opportunities will be available for you. If you choose not to take advantage of the opportunities you are given, not just education, you will later in life realize your foolishness.

Today think about your life. Are you content with the way it is flowing? Do you understand all you care to know? Have you accomplished all you want to accomplish? I feel the more you learn, the more you want to know. Also, the more you accomplish, the more you want to accomplish. Be aware today of anything of which you are not certain and strive for more understanding. Discipline yourself to continue to learn and understand. Do not be foolish and live in ignorance of all there is to learn, especially God's Word. Each of you has so much potential. Discipline yourself to be wise and enjoy the fountain of a wonderful life, not a fool and waste your precious gift.

Very rarely will anyone die for a righteous person, though for a good person someone might possibly dare to die. But God demonstrates His own love toward us, in that while we were yet sinners, Christ died for us. Romans 5:7-8 (New International Version)

I have always been so grateful and maybe even taken for granted that Jesus died for me and for you. As I was reading this verse, I realized Jesus also died for the very people who beat Him and hung Him on the cross. He asked God to forgive them for they did not know what they were doing. Many times I find it hard to even do something nice for someone who has hurt one my loved ones or me. Jesus didn't look around and see really good people and think He would die so they could keep on being nice. No, He died because He knew this was God's plan for Him. He died so we all would be forgiven of our sins and have everlasting life. All we have to do is believe Jesus Christ is the Son of God, who died for us, arose on the third day and is alive today! We should live in a way deserving of the sacrifice Jesus made for all of us, sinners as we are. We should love and accept others because of the wonderful example Jesus set for us because He loved us first.

Today do something nice for someone who has hurt you. It may just be a smile or a kind word. That's a start. Remember what Jesus did for you. Make Him smile because you followed His example. We must not let Jesus' death be in vain.

When you give to the poor, don't let your left hand know what your right hand is doing. Matthew 6:3 (God's Word® Translation)

The sixth chapter of Matthew is one of my favorite chapters in the Bible. I really should read it every day. It covers just about everything we need to know to handle life as we should and to help us through the day. Jesus made it very clear that we are not to be showoffs. Sometimes I feel people who brag about what they have done and how good they are can cause more damage to the Christian faith than anyone. People will know you are a Christian, not because you tell them, but because you live as one. We should give to others and do for others because it is the right thing to do, not so everyone will think we are such a wonderful person. Yes, it is okay to talk about your faith. In fact, it is very important that we share our faith. We just need to always be aware if we are doing this for others and not for ourselves. I love this quote from Dwight L. Moody. "Character is what man is in the dark."

Today be aware of the needs of those around you. When you see someone in need make every effort to help them without asking for any praise. Learn to feel the joy of giving rather than the pride of praise. Giving of yourself is the best gift ever, and it doesn't cost a penny.

(Xerxes), the king, loved Esther more than all the other women. She won more favor and approval from him than did any of the other young women. He placed the royal crown on her head and made her queen in place of Vashti. Esther 2:17 (HCSB)

Because the Jews were hated by many at the time Esther was chosen to be Queen, she had not revealed to anyone in the palace that she was Jewish. When Esther learned the king's chief advisor was scheming to kill all the Jews of Persia, she went to her cousin, Mordecai, who had adopted her after the death of her parents. He told her if she remained silent all of her fellow Jews would be killed. He also called it to her attention that she may have been placed in her royal position by God for such a time as this. Because of Esther's faith in God and her acceptance of her responsibility, she risked her life by going to the king on behalf of the Jewish people. Because of Esther's bravery, her people were saved. This story reminds me of the many times in my own life, I have seen God place people in a position to help others or to be helped. He has definitely put me in places where I have been helped. Because I was in Florida when I had my dissected aorta, God was able to use Dr. Michael DeFrain to save my life. Ironically, Dr. DeFrain used a procedure pioneered by Dr. Michael Debakey, a famous heart surgeon at the Texas Heart Institute in Houston, Texas, who had saved Poppa's father's life in 1967. God also gave me Dr. Mohamed Ali, a pulmonologist, who took care of me during this horrible time. Both Dr. Defrain and Dr. Ali were so kind to your poppa and parents when I was so ill. Poppa and I are going to miss both of these special doctors and great men when we move back to Tennessee. We will forever be grateful that God placed them into our lives.

Today and always, be aware of the needs of those around you. Like Esther, God may place you in the right place at the right time.

Your word is a lamp for my feet and a light on my path. Psalms 119:105 (Holman Christian Standard Bible)

How many times do you stumble when walking in complete darkness? We are always glad to find a flashlight. The great lesson in this verse is that God's word is a light for our life. We all stumble with many trials in life. The Bible has the answer. Go to one of the Bible verses you have learned or read your Bible and see if you find encouraging words. Some Bibles have a section which tells you where to go for different situations. Most importantly, go straight to God. He is always there to light your path and to put an answer on your heart if you will listen.

Today when something is bothering you go to your Bible. The answer will be there, or at least the comfort of God's word will help you see the light at the end of the tunnel. It will guide your way. Until you see that light, trust God and the light of His glory and grace to lead you through.

....(Be) Zealous for the fear of the Lord. Proverbs 23:17 (New International Version)

The first of this verse tells us not to let our heart envy sinners. I don't know why I thought of this incident in my life, but I think I will share it with you as an example. When I was in my late teens I was working as a secretary; and, for the first time ever, I was not under the supervision of my mother or teachers. Two of my co-workers were very carefree and did and said exactly what they wanted. My mother had always stressed to me I should be nice and considerate of others. I found myself impressed by their behavior. One day a friend of Mother's was with us and I just didn't feel like being nice. I wasn't. I will never forget the look on her face and on Mother's. I felt terrible. I had not only disappointed my mother and her friend, my conscience told me I had disappointed my God. I knew then I never wanted to act like that again. Fear of the Lord is good. In fact, it is what God wants. When you fear someone don't you strive to please them? God doesn't want us to fear Him just to make Him feel important. He wants us to fear Him and be zealous to please Him because He knows His way is best for us.

Today check your conscience. Are you ever afraid you are not pleasing your parents? Are you envious of people who don't seem to worry about their actions? Do you care how God feels about your actions? How good do you feel when you know everyone is pleased with your actions? Think about your answers. If you don't really care if you are doing right, you should change your attitude with zeal. Don't delay. You will find the more you are eager to please God, the easier it becomes and the happier and more content your life will be. It has been said a person becomes wise when watching what happens to him when he isn't.

Chapter Two

A gentle answer turns away wrath, but a harsh word stirs up anger. Proverbs 15:1 (New International Version)

A fool always loses his temper, but a wise man holds it back. Proverbs 29:11 (New American Standard Bible)

Solomon, the author of these proverbs, was a very wise man. Too often tempers flare and nothing is solved, when holding back anger and speaking gently about the problem would bring about a solution. Some people seem to enjoy causing friction among others and never say a kind word. Others are almost always kind and considerate of everyone. It certainly isn't easy to be kind and calm all the time. Harsh words seem to come much easier than a gentle answer. Remembering the above Proverbs is something we all should do. Imagine how peaceful life would be if we all would think before we speak, always giving kind answers and holding back the bad thoughts we have. I have really been working on this and it is not easy. I found counting to ten (or even to a hundred) doesn't always work, but when I immediately ask God to either quieten me or give me the right words, it seems to come easier. Be selective in your battles. Sometimes peace is better than being right.

Today notice how your words or the words of others determine the mood of the day. Before you say something, think of how you would feel if someone said it to you. Be aware and take pride in the times you stop yourself before you speak harshly. Are you the type of person who turns away wrath and brings joy to your life and to the life of those around you?

Blessed be the God and Father of our Lord Jesus Christ, the Father of mercies and God of all comfort; who comforts us in all our troubles, so that we can comfort those in any trouble with the comfort we ourselves receive from God. 2 Corinthians 1:3-4 (English Standard Version)

God of Comfort. I love that thought. I have felt God's comfort many times in my life, but I have felt it more the older I get. Many times I have been given the ability to comfort others because of the times God comforted me through the same trials they are now facing. So much pain and sadness cannot really be understood unless you have been through it yourself. Then you are able to truly identify with some, not all, of the feelings others are having and be of comfort to them.

Today be aware of those around you. Are they in need of comfort? Have you felt as they do, and what helped you at those times? Was it someone just listening and caring, or did someone do or say something to you that may be comforting to someone else? Most importantly, always remember to pray for those needing comfort. Who does God want you praying for right now?

Come to Me, all of you who are weary and burdened, and I will give you rest. Matthew 11:28 (New International Version)

Isn't it a wonderful feeling to know when you are sad and troubled God invites you to come to Him and promises to give you rest? Don't turn down this special invitation. This may sound too simple. I didn't say He would solve your problem, but He will give you strength and suggestions (thoughts) to handle whatever comes your way. You may also realize your problem is not as bad as you thought, and it will soon pass to another problem you and God will handle. Yes, life does have a lot of ups and downs. Just don't let the downs keep you from loving life and enjoying the wonderful ups. Learn to make your first instinct in every situation be to turn to God for an answer.

Today when you have something on your mind causing you worry or unhappiness go to a quiet place and talk to God. Tell Him everything. He will not tell your secrets. Then listen. I promise you will feel better if you truly turn your problem over to God. The more you do this, the easier it becomes. Sometimes when things seem to be falling apart, they may actually be falling in place.

Do everything without complaining and arguing. Philippians 2:14 (New Living Translation)

This is certainly good advice but not all that easy to follow. It is easy for me to avoid arguing because it is so unpleasant for me to even be around arguments. However, I am bad to complain about all my aches and pains when I should thank God, every day that I am alive to have these feelings. As I waste my breath complaining about life, someone out there is taking their last breath. Some people complain about everything. Nothing ever satisfies them. Complaining only emphasizes the problem and keeps you from appreciating the good. When something bothers you change it, accept it or leave the situation. All else causes nothing but unhappiness. "The pessimist complains about the wind. The optimist expects it to change. The realist adjusts the sails." William A. Ward....... Which one are you?

Today be aware of every time you complain or argue. Also, ask yourself if this solved anything. How do you feel when you listen to a complainer or are involved in an argument? Isn't it better to be around pleasant people? Are you one of those pleasant people? Focusing on the good is a much better way to rejoice and be glad in the day God has given you. Try it and see if you agree.

Enter through the narrow gate. For wide is the gate and broad is the road that leads to destruction and many enter through it. But small is the gate and narrow is the road that leads to life, and only a few find it. Matthew 7:13-14 (New International Version)

It seems too often the way of life accepted by the majority of people is not the path we should take. It is so much easier to go with the crowd through that wide gate leading to destruction than to enter the narrow gate which symbolizes the discipline to do God's will. One of the quotes I had saved says it best: "A lie doesn't become truth, wrong doesn't become right and evil doesn't become good just because it is accepted by a majority." (Rick Warren) This is why it is so important to go to God's word each day and to discipline ourselves to live according to His will. It may be more fun and easier at the time to follow the crowd, but you will find that easy is not always best. Following God's will through the small gate and narrow road not only prevents bad consequences to our disobedience, but it also leads to an eternal paradise. "God never said the journey would be easy, but He did say that the arrival will be worthwhile." (Max Lucado)

Today when you begin to make a choice ask yourself, "Which gate am I entering…the road to life or the road to destruction?"

For unto you is born this day in the City of David a Savior, who is Christ the Lord. Luke 2:11 (English Standard Version)

When I read this scripture, of course, I think of Christmas and the Christmas story. But think about it. That was the day God sent His Son to us. It has been over 2000 years and He is still alive. Maybe not on this earth, but watching over us. Jesus only lived on earth thirty-three years. He died a painful death on the cross so our sins would be forgiven. By His example and His words during those few years He lived among us, we were shown how to live our lives in a way pleasing to God. If we accept Jesus as our Lord and Savior, we are promised to live forever with Him in Paradise (Heaven). What a great Christmas present!!!!

Today try to follow Jesus' example. When in doubt while making a decision or while just talking with others ask yourself, "What would Jesus do or say?" Jesus will always be there when you need Him. What a wonderful feeling to know our Savior, born in a manger so many years ago, LIVES today within our hearts.

Give thanks to the LORD, for he is good, for his steadfast love endures forever. Psalms 136:1 (English Standard Version)

Forever…now that is a long time. I remember when I was your age I thought 30 was really old. Now at 74, when I hear of someone 90 I think they are really old and 74 seems pretty young. Even now it is hard for me to envision forever. I have no problem knowing God's love has been with me my entire life, even at the times I was not giving God the praise and appreciation He deserves. This verse speaks clearly. God's love endures forever. We are promised a life "forever" in Heaven with our Lord and Savior and all of our loved ones, "If you confess with your mouth that Jesus is Lord and believe in your heart that God raised him from the dead, you will be saved." Romans 10:9 (New Living Translation) What a wonderful gift! We have been blessed throughout our lives with so many gifts from God, and we should remember to give thanks and love to God "forever" for God is good!

Today be aware of your blessings. I first planned to suggest you keep a note pad near and write them down when you see or think of one. I then decided if you did that you would miss a lot of your blessings because you would be too busy writing. A better plan is to enjoy your blessings. If you have a good attitude, I promise you will find a lot more blessings than complaints. Remember to give thanks to God and love Him as He loves you.

He is not here: for he is risen, as he said. Come, see the place where the Lord lay. Matthew 28:6 (New International Version)

He is risen indeed!!! This verse is in one of the beautiful Easter stories in the Bible which tells of Jesus' resurrection, the cornerstone of Christianity. What emotions Mary Magdalene and the other Mary must have felt that morning when the angel spoke to them. The angel also told them not to be afraid, just as Jesus had told His followers many times. This was the emotional end and beginning for Jesus. It was the end of all His suffering for us on earth and the beginning of His going to be with His Father in heaven to prepare a place for all who believe in Him.

Today be aware that our Savior is not dead. He is risen and is very much alive. Feel Him beside you every step of the way. Is He glad to be there? Make Him proud and have a great day with your friend, Jesus.

Please read the following pages of Grandmomma's thoughts and more information about Easter. Don't let the number of pages scare you. Even Poppa said it is interesting.

Thoughts about Easter

As I write these thoughts, Poppa is now home recuperating from a total knee replacement. We came home from the hospital on Easter Sunday. It is only the second time either of us has not been in church on Easter Sunday. The other time was when we took Lea Ellen and Darren to Disney on Spring Break when they were very young. In fact, it may have been the year Disney in Florida opened. We both decided then we would never miss church on Easter again. It just didn't feel right. This time we didn't have a choice. The doctor worked Poppa in for surgery because he was in such pain. While we were at the hospital we were able to talk with many of the employees about their plans for Easter. Some had to work, even though they would rather be with their families at church. Others were treating it as any other day or planning a big meal and Easter egg hunt or just enjoying the candy. What surprised us the most was the stories we heard of how many people do not even know what Easter is all about, much less Shrove Tuesday, Ash Wednesday, Lent, Maundy Thursday and Good Friday. Do you? Of course, if you go to church you have heard the true Easter story, not about the Easter Bunny. You have also learned about it if you go to a church affiliated school. Public schools are not allowed to even mention Jesus.

I am going to do the best I can to explain the days of the Easter Season. When I looked for help on the computer, there was too much detail for my simple mind. It also seemed there were more sites about Easter recipes and other non-religious celebrations than the real Easter meanings. It was only when I became concerned about the people who do not know the reasons for the days of this season that I realized how little I knew. There is so much information on the Internet and I sort of bottom-lined what I found most interesting. Please do some extensive studying on your own, as there is so much to learn and then share with the ones who do not know. You may even be able to give Poppa a quiz he won't be able to answer.

Easter is really an entire season of the Christian church year. The week preceding Easter is called Holy Week and includes Maundy Thursday, which commemorates Jesus' last supper with his disciples; Good Friday, which honors the day of his crucifixion; and Holy Saturday, which focuses on the transition between the crucifixion and resurrection. The word "Easter" does not appear in the Bible and no early church celebrations of Christ's resurrection are mentioned in Scripture. Easter, like Christmas, is a tradition that developed later in church history.

Lent is a forty-day period of fasting leading up to Easter, excluding Sundays because Sunday is the day of the Resurrection and is skipped over when calculating the length of Lent. The purpose is to set aside time for reflection on Jesus Christ - his suffering and his sacrifice, his life, death, burial and resurrection. By observing the forty days of Lent, the individual Christian imitates the forty days Jesus spent in the wilderness fasting and being tempted by the devil (Luke 4:2). Some churches put more emphasis on the fasting than others. Originally, "Lent" was nothing more than the English name of the season between winter and summer, the season when the snow melts and the flowers bloom. The church's observance of the resurrection of Christ took place during the season of lent. In England, "Lent" came to mean the observance rather than the season, leaving the season without a name. Instead of saying stupid things like "Lent happens during lent," English-speaking people invented the word "spring." Lent can be viewed as a spiritual spring cleaning: a time for taking spiritual inventory and then cleaning out those things which interfere with our relationships with Jesus Christ and our service to Him. Some Christians who observe lent make a commitment to give up something--a habit, such as smoking, swearing, watching too much TV, or a food or drink, such as sweets, chocolate or coffee. By giving these up, the person fasting learns to control a part of his or her life, which leads to greater self-discipline even when Lent is over. Some Christians also take on a Lenten discipline, such as reading the Bible and spending more time in prayer, preparing their hearts for the wonderful Easter morning when our Lord and Savior, Jesus Christ, arose from the grave. He lives!!!!!

Shrove Tuesday is the day before Ash Wednesday, the beginning of Lent in the Roman Catholic Church (and those Protestant churches that observe Lent). Shrove is the past tense of the word shrive, which means to hear a confession, assign penance, and absolve from sin. In the Middle Ages, especially in Northern Europe and England, it became the custom to confess one's sins on the day before Lent began in order to enter the season in the right spirit. Shrove Tuesday was originally a solemn day; but over the centuries, in anticipation of the Lenten fast that would begin the next day, Shrove Tuesday took on a festive nature. That is why Shrove Tuesday, also known as Fat Tuesday or Mardi Gras (which is simply French for Fat Tuesday), is celebrated as a last hurrah of food and fun before the fasting begins. For centuries, it was customary to fast by abstaining from meat during Lent, which is why some people call the festival Carnival, which is Latin for farewell to meat. Many churches traditionally celebrate Shrove Tuesday by serving pancakes symbolizing using up rich foods such as eggs and dairy products in anticipation of the 40-day fasting season of Lent.

Ash Wednesday marks the first day, or the start of the season of Lent. Not all Christians celebrate Ash Wednesday. Actually, it is mainly celebrated by Catholics, as well as Lutherans, Methodists, Presbyterians, and Anglicans. On Ash Wednesday Christians go to church to receive ash on their foreheads. It is often a day of fasting. What most people notice on Ash Wednesday is that an awful lot of Christians are running around with ashes smudged on their foreheads. The ashes are made from the blessed palms used in the Palm Sunday celebration from the year prior. They are christened with Holy Water and are scented by incense. They are a symbol of repentance and sincere remorse for wrongdoing; which is why believers are told "Remember, Man is dust, and unto dust you shall return" when he/she receives the ashes. While throughout the day the ashes may turn into more of a smudge, they are actually applied to the forehead as the sign of the cross.

Palm Sunday, often referred to as "Passion Sunday," marks the beginning of Holy Week and the last week of Lent. Some 450 to 500 years prior to Jesus' arrival in Jerusalem, the prophet Zechariah had prophesied the event we now call Palm Sunday: "Rejoice, O people of Zion! Shout in triumph, O people of Jerusalem! Look, your king is coming to you. He is righteous and victorious, yet he is humble, riding on a donkey--riding on a donkey's colt." (Zechariah 9:9 NLV) The prophecy was fulfilled in every way, and it was truly a time of rejoicing, as Jerusalem welcomed their King. Unfortunately, the celebration was not to last. The crowds looked for a Messiah who would rescue them politically and free them nationally, but Jesus had come to save them spiritually. First things first, and mankind's primary need is spiritual, not political, cultural, or national salvation. Palm Sunday was the day Jesus made His triumphant entry into Jerusalem, knowing that this journey would end in his sacrificial death on the cross for the sins of all mankind. Before he entered Jerusalem, he sent two of his disciples to a village ahead of them and told them where they would find a young donkey which had never been ridden. He told them, "If anyone asks you, 'Why are you untying it?' say, 'The Lord needs it.' (Luke 19:31 NIV) The men brought the donkey to Jesus, and placed their cloaks on its back. The symbolism of the donkey may refer to the Eastern tradition that it is an animal of peace, versus the horse, which is the animal of war. Jesus humbly entered Jerusalem riding on a donkey, not as a war-waging king but as the Prince of Peace. The people greeted Him enthusiastically, waving palm branches and covering his path with palm branches and shouting: "Hosanna to the Son of David: Blessed is he that cometh in the name of the Lord; Hosanna in the highest." (Matthew 21:9 KJB) The shouts of "Hosanna" meant "save now," and the palm branches symbolized goodness and victory. Interestingly, at the end of the Bible, people will wave palm branches once again to praise and honor Jesus Christ: "After this I looked, and there before me was a great multitude that no one could count, from every nation, tribe, people and language, standing before the throne and before the Lamb. They were wearing white robes and were holding palm branches in their hands." (Revelation 7:9 NIV)

Maundy Thursday, also known as "Holy Thursday," is the day on which Jesus celebrated the Passover with His disciples, known as the Last Supper. Only hours after the Last Supper, Judas would betray Christ in the Garden of Gethsemane, setting the stage for Christ's Crucifixion on Good Friday. Two important events are the focus of Maundy Thursday. First, Jesus celebrated the Last Supper with His disciples; and this was the beginning of the Lord's Supper, also called Communion. Some Christian churches have a special Communion service on Maundy Thursday in memory of Jesus' Last Supper with His disciples. Second, Jesus washed the disciples' feet as an act of humility and service, setting an example that we should humbly love and serve one another. (John 13:3-17). Some Christian churches observe a foot-washing ceremony on Maundy Thursday to commemorate Jesus' washing the feet of the disciples. The word Maundy comes from the Latin word for "command." The "Maundy" in "Maundy Thursday" refers to the command Jesus gave to the disciples on that night. After they had finished the meal, as they walked into the night toward Gethsemane, Jesus taught his disciples a "new" commandment that was not really new: "I give you a new command: Love one another. Just as I have loved you, you must also love one another. "John 13:34-35 (Holman Christian Standard Bible)

Good Friday, the Friday before Easter Sunday, is the most difficult day of Holy Week. It is the day on which Jesus Christ, having been betrayed by Judas and sentenced to death by Pontius Pilate, was crucified for the sins of mankind. According to Scripture, Judas Iscariot, the disciple who had betrayed Jesus, was overcome with guilt and hanged himself early Friday morning.

Meanwhile, before the third hour (9 a.m.), Jesus endured the shame of false accusations, condemnation, mockery, beatings, and abandonment. After multiple unlawful trials, He was sentenced to death by crucifixion, one of the most horrible and disgraceful methods of capital punishment. Before Christ was led away, soldiers spit on him, tormented and mocked him, and pierced him with a crown of thorns. Then Jesus carried his own cross to Calvary where, again, he was mocked and insulted as Roman soldiers nailed him to the wooden cross.

Jesus spoke seven final statements from the cross. Then, about the ninth hour (3 p.m.), Jesus breathed his last and died. By 6 p.m. Friday evening, Nicodemus and Joseph of Arimathea, took Jesus' body down from the cross and lay it in a tomb

There are many opinions as to why Good Friday is called Good since it is a day of torture and sadness. In the end, the historical origins of why Good Friday is called Good Friday remain unclear, but the theological reason is very likely the one expressed by the Baltimore Catechism: Good Friday is good because the death of Christ, as terrible as it was, led to the Resurrection on Easter Sunday, which brought new life to those who believe. The goodness of God and the Good News—the Gospel—is rooted in the cross. The sacrificial death of Christ at Calvary is the means by which God pours the blessings of His goodness into our lives, and that's why the phrase Good Friday is improbably appropriate. The cross is the crux of God's plan of redemption and predominant in the heart and soul of Christians everywhere.

The Last Statements of Jesus

Jesus spoke these seven final statements from the cross:

"Father, forgive them, for they do not know what they are doing. Luke 23:34 (New International Version)

"Truly I tell you, today you will be with me in paradise." Luke 23:43 (New International Version)

When Jesus saw his mother there, and the disciple whom he loved standing nearby, he said to her, "Woman, here is your son," and to the disciple, "Here is your mother." From that time on, this disciple took her into his home. John 19:26-27 (New International Version)

"My God, my God, why have you forsaken me?"
Matthew 27:46 (New International Version)
Mark 15:34 (New International Version)

"I thirst." John 19:28 (English Standard Version)

"It is finished!" John 19:30 (New International Version)

"Father, into your hands I commit my spirit." When he had said this, he breathed his last. "Luke 23:46 (New International Version)

Holy Saturday is the day between Good Friday and Easter Sunday. It commemorates the day when Jesus Christ lay in the tomb after his death. It is also known as Easter Eve or Black Saturday and is the final day of Lent. Many Christians in the United States attend an Easter vigil service on Holy Saturday. Candles that are used for Easter vigil services represent the light of Jesus Christ, and the realization that he brings light into darkness. An Easter candle is also lit in some homes, particularly among families who cannot attend the Easter vigil services.

Many American families prepare for Easter Sunday celebrations on the Saturday before Easter. For Christians, the egg is a symbol of Jesus' resurrection, as when they are cracked open they stand for the empty tomb. No-one actually knows when eggs were first used as symbols at festival times but it was long before Jesus' time. Eggs were always thought to be special because although they do not seem alive, they have life within them, especially at springtime when chicks hatch out. Children decorate hard boiled eggs with water colors, stickers and other material. These eggs are often placed in Easter baskets. There are many accounts as to how dying eggs became a part of the tradition surrounding the Christian holiday of Easter, but nothing definite. Some people give chocolate eggs as gifts this time of the year. The egg itself is a symbol of the Resurrection while being dormant it contains a new life sealed within it. The custom of giving eggs at Easter celebrates new life. Christians remember that Jesus, after dying on the cross, rose from the dead. This miracle showed that life could win over death. The story of the Easter Bunny is thought to have become common in the 19th century. Rabbits usually give birth to a big litter of babies (called kittens), so they became a symbol of new life. Even if your church does not recognize Holy Saturday, it is a wonderful tradition to follow, enjoying the Easter Celebration and always remembering the life, death and resurrection of our Lord and Savior, Jesus Christ.

Easter Sunday is the day Christians celebrate Jesus Christ's resurrection from the grave. It is typically the best attended Sunday service of the year for Christian churches. Christians believe, according to Scripture, that Jesus came back to life, or was raised from the dead, three days after his death on the cross. Through his death, burial, and resurrection, Jesus paid the penalty for sin, thus purchasing for all who believe in him, eternal life in Christ Jesus.

Because of Easter's non-religious traditions, and also because of the commercialization of Easter, many Christian churches choose to refer to this Easter holiday as Resurrection Day. Easter Sunday marks the end of Lent and the Easter season. The miracle of the resurrection, described in the Bible, is the most important miracle of the Christian faith. When Jesus Christ rose from the dead on the first Easter morning, He showed people that the hope He proclaimed in His Gospel message was real, and so was God's power at work in the world. The resurrection miracle gives all people in this fallen world hope that their suffering can lead to joy.

Where to Find the Story of Easter in the Bible

The Bible does not mention Ash Wednesday or the custom of Lent, however, the practice of repentance and mourning in ashes is found in 2 Samuel 13:19; Esther 4:1; Job 2:8; Daniel 9:3; and Matthew 11:21.

The biblical account of Palm Sunday can be found in Matthew 21:1-11; Mark 11:1-11; Luke 19:28-4 and John 12:12-19.

Maundy Thursday – The Last Supper - can be found in Matthew 26:17-30; Mark 14:12-25; Luke 22:7-20.

The biblical account of Jesus' death on the cross, or crucifixion, his burial and his resurrection, or raising from the dead, can be found in the following passages of Scripture: Matthew 27:27-28:8; Mark 15:16-16:19; Luke 23:26-24:35; and John 19:16-20:30.

All four of the Bible's Gospel (which means "good news") books - Matthew, Mark, Luke, and John -- describe the good news that angels announced on the first Easter: Jesus had risen from the dead, just as he told his disciples he would three days after his crucifixion. "For just as Jonah was three days and three nights in the belly of the great fish, so will the Son of Man be three days and three nights in the heart of the earth." (ESV) Matthew 12:40

In your anger do not sin. Do not let the sun go down while you are still angry. Ephesians 4:26 (New International Version)

When you are mad, do you want to do something nice? Now that's a stupid question. No, we want to hurt whoever hurt us. That is a sin according to so many lessons Jesus taught, but it is such a natural reaction. We are human. We may need to walk away from the situation for a while, but to carry anger over for days and days causes us to waste so much of our life with a heavy load on our heart. You cannot change how people treat you or how they talk about you. All you can change is how you react to it. I always worry something will happen and I will never be able to make peace with the one with whom I am angry. I have kept Poppa up many nights until we settled a disagreement. I think he might have said it was settled just so he could go to sleep.

Today find a way to handle your anger. Is the situation that important? Did you have any part in the problem? If not, how can you find peace in the situation? Sometimes it is the person causing the problem who should be in our prayers. It is usually someone unhappy who is not content to see others happy. Communication is so important. Poppa and your parents have casually mentioned things I have done that got on their nerves many years ago, and I didn't have a clue. I now try not to do those same things they have put up with for years. Think how much happier they would have been if we had communicated and I had stopped it earlier. Of course, you do need to be tactful in your communications. Remember this scripture and pray God will help you find forgiveness in your heart. A true sign of maturity is when someone hurts you and you try to understand their situation instead of hurting them back. What have I always said? Two wrongs don't make a right.

Jesus said to Thomas, "You believe because you've seen me. Blessed are those who haven't seen me but believe." John 20:29 (God's Word® Translation)

Thomas was Jesus' disciple who doubted His resurrection from the grave until he was able to place his hand in Jesus' wounds. Are you a doubting Thomas? We have information Thomas did not have. We have the Bible telling the rest of the story. Even with the Bible, the world is full of skeptics who do not believe because they have not seen. They find it hard to believe all the miracles of Jesus, especially that He arose from the dead. There is a feeling inside of me which causes me to be able to do nothing but believe. It must be the Holy Spirit. Jesus said He would not leave us alone. When we believe in Him the Holy Spirit lives forever within us. That is why all Jesus wants us to do is believe in Him and have faith we will see Him again. We haven't seen Jesus, but we are blessed because we know He lives.

Today test yourself. Do you really believe? If you have any doubts, maybe you should read about Doubting Thomas in John 20:24-29. If you really want to know about the faith shown by others in the Bible, take time today to read about faith in action in Hebrew 11. I also have faith in all of you. I know you will do whatever it takes to become whatever you choose to be and will do it well, with God's help.

Keep your tongue from evil, and your lips from speaking lies. Psalm 34:13 (New Heart English Bible)

Television shows, movies and songs of today are filled with cursing and actions less than pleasing to God. This is contagious. It has become a natural way of life for so many. When you are around someone who chooses to use foul language, it is tempting to do the same. If you are around someone who likes to gossip and say deceitful things about others, sometimes it is tempting to join them. Gossip not only is wrong, it is very dangerous. Many lives have been ruined because of lies told about them. It is also tempting to try to deceive others to make ourselves look good or innocent. This is when you need to remember this verse.

Today watch your mouth. Do not say words you should not. Tell the truth and do not try to deceive anyone. If you always tell the truth you won't have to remember what you said. Do not speak evil to or about others. In fact, try to spread kindness. It is contagious also. Choose your friends wisely then you will be sure to catch the right attitude.

Let us not become weary in doing good, for at the proper time we will reap a harvest if we do not give up. Galatians 6:9 (New International Version)

Throughout my life I have known people who seem to always be aware of others' needs and are always more than willing to help. They are not looking for praise or rewards. They are just good people, whom I truly admire. This verse is much more difficult for me than you would think. I truly love doing good for others and love the joy I feel from doing this. I do, however, sometimes become weary. It seems I enjoy doing good deeds for others when it is my idea and not when it is expected of me. This is a verse I am glad I chose, and I think I will write it on a piece of paper and carry it with me as a reminder. I am so glad God doesn't grow weary doing good for me.

Today try to enjoy all the good deeds you do. When you become weary of requests for help from others remember this verse. Don't give up. Know at the proper time you will reap a wonderful harvest, and God will tell you face to face, "Well done, good and faithful servant!" (Matt. 25:21 NIV).

"My thoughts are nothing like your thoughts," says the Lord. "And my ways are far beyond anything you can imagine. Isaiah 55:8 (New Living Translation)

This verse tells us why it is so important for us to turn our problems, as well as our dreams, over to God. He is aware of every situation in our lives, good or bad. He has everything under control. I don't always understand His thoughts or His ways when in a situation, but I usually see his reasoning after the fact and realize it was for the good. I will admit I still have so many things I do not understand. That is because God's thoughts are different from mine and His reasons are also better. I hope He won't mind if I do ask a few questions when I see Him in heaven. On second thought, it doesn't really matter what I think. God is in control and He knows what He is doing without my opinion.

Today when you are making a decision think about what God might do with the same decision. Ask Him about it. Listen in your heart to what you think God would say. Then make your best decision. If it's wrong, that's okay. You learned and God will help you through anything.

Nothing in all creation is hidden from God's sight. Everything is uncovered and laid bare before the eyes of Him to whom we must give account. Hebrews 4:13 (New International Version)

Everywhere you go now someone has a camera watching. Cell phone cameras or security cameras are everywhere. Even with all the cameras, there are still places you can go where no one can see. This is not so with God. We are never hidden from His sight. This is both a comforting and a disturbing thought. It is wonderful to know God is watching when you are in trouble, but sometimes I do things I wish God didn't see. This verse helps me think twice before I do something displeasing to God.

Today be aware you are never hidden from God's sight. You are on His permanent security camera. Does He like what he sees?

Open your mouth for the mute, for the rights of all the unfortunate. Open your mouth, judge righteously, and defend the rights of the afflicted and needy. Proverbs 31:8-9 (New American Standard Bible)

I don't think this verse really means we need to march on the streets or go to Congress to defend the rights of the unfortunate, but I think it does remind us we should care. Of course, rules have been changed for the rights of others by people who go the extra mile to get it done. That is a good choice we can make. I feel we can also help the unfortunate by just being alert. When we see someone in need we should do our best to help. Sometimes the only thing we can do is pray. Prayer is a powerful helper. It may also give you an idea of how you can help that person or another person you may come upon in the future.

Today be aware of the unfortunate you see and pray you will do what you can for them or others like them. It is so sad in this day and time, as it has probably always been, safety is a consideration when dealing with a stranger. With that in mind, don't forget to pray and do the best you can. No one can help everyone, but everyone can help someone. Keep your eyes and heart opened for those in need. You may also find people you know who could use your help and prayers.

Praise the Lord in song for He has done excellent things. Let this be known throughout the earth. Isaiah 12:5 (New American Standard 1977)

I love to sing. Poppa and I love to sing in church where voices join together to praise God. It is amazing how singing a song of praise can lift your spirits and brighten your day. Isiah encouraged God's people to not only sing their personal praise to God for all He had done for them, but to also let it be known to others throughout the earth. When you praise the Lord in song or with a joyful attitude, others will be encouraged to do the same. Our world seems to be more and more filled with people who are so discouraged and without hope. Of course, just singing a happy song or having a happy attitude is not going to solve any problems. However, sometimes it may give a little bit of happiness and encouragement to an otherwise hopeless situation.

Today praise the Lord in song. I know sometimes my singing drives you crazy. It certainly did your parents. But even your parents would eventually smile at my silliness. You don't have to drive others crazy, but sing enough to bring joy to your own heart. Then share it with others. I know your singing always brings joy to my life. God has given each of you a beautiful voice. Use that voice to praise the One from whom it came.

Quicken me after thy loving kindness, so shall I keep the testimony of thy mouth. Psalm 119:88 (American King James Version)

Psalm 119 is an Acrostic Psalm, which means it is written in the Hebrew alphabetical order. It was when I read about these psalms years ago I got the idea of memorizing verses in alphabetical order, which led to my writing this book. There are many translations of this verse, but I chose this one because it starts with a Q. "Quicken" is translated most often as "revive". However, I liked God's Word translation which reads, "Give me a new life through your mercy so that I may obey the written instructions, [which came] from your mouth." This verse speaks for itself. We all are given the privilege of starting our life anew. Our God is a God of second chances. We are encouraged in a new life by studying His word and learning the instructions which have been given us to assure our new life is the life God has chosen for us.

Today ask God to help renew your life so you will show His loving kindness and remember His teachings. It might be a good day to remember some of your previously learned verses and see how many you can follow today.

Rejoice in the Lord always. Again, I will say rejoice. Philippians 4:4 (New International Version)

Rejoice. We all love to rejoice and be happy. In fact, that is a normal reaction when things are going well. However, the apostle Paul wrote this scripture while he was in prison awaiting trial. He did not know whether he would be released or killed. So why rejoice? It certainly wasn't his circumstances. If Paul's attitude was based on his horrible circumstances, he would have no earthly reason to rejoice. Paul had learned to place his reasons for rejoicing on more solid ground. His purpose, his meaning in life, his reason for being content and thankful is founded upon nothing else but his faith in Jesus Christ. With Christ, you cannot lose. He will be with you on earth and has prepared a beautiful place for you when your life on earth is over. Rejoice!

Today try to look for the best in everything that happens and make it a learning experience. This morning my computer wasn't working and I was not rejoicing. Poppa fixed it and I realized how nice it is to have a computer and someone to fix it. I do definitely realize Paul's circumstances should not be compared to computer problems. I just mean if we strive to rejoice always in every situation, we will be ready when the big trials come. Sometimes the reason for rejoicing does not come quickly, but we can rejoice in knowing God is with us in all situations and will use everything for our good if we love and trust Him.

So watch yourselves. "If your brother or sister sins against you, rebuke them. And if they repent, forgive them. Even if they sin against you seven times in a day and seven times come back to you saying, 'I repent', you must forgive them." Luke 17:3-4 (New International Version)

If we are honest, most of us do not like this scripture. It is probably one of the hardest things to do. Jesus definitely practiced what He preached. He didn't just forgive us. He died so we would always be forgiven. I find when I pray for the one who hurt me, I realize they really need pity more than forgiveness. Everyone makes bad mistakes in life; however, that doesn't mean they have to pay for them the rest of their lives. Sometimes good people make bad choices. That doesn't mean they are bad. It means they are human. I also find when I can forgive and move on with my life I am much more at peace and able to enjoy each day without dwelling on the past. If I am honest with myself, I know I have done some things I should not have done more than once and God continues to forgive me. Oh, how I pray I can do the same.

Today be aware of the people you are having trouble forgiving. Pray for God's help in giving you understanding, forgiveness and then move on with the life God wishes for you. See how much better you feel. Remember, forgiving does not change the past. It changes the future. Most of all, forgive because Jesus gave His life on the cross so we all could be forgiven.

Trust in the Lord with all your heart and lean not on your own understanding. In all your ways acknowledge Him and He will direct your paths. Proverbs 3:5-6 (New American Standard Bible)

This is a very important scripture for me. Too often in my life I have not understood why things have happened. This verse reminds me I don't need to understand. I just need to trust the Lord. He knows. I have seen so many times I trusted God to help me and He definitely did. He used the situation for my good and had a purpose in mind to guide me and lead me in the direction I should go. God is faithful. We must learn to live by promises, not by explanations. Yes, I do not need to understand. I just need to trust and obey.

Today think about the events of your life, both good and bad, and look deeply for some good that has happened because of it. Sometimes the only good you may find is the lesson you learned so you will not repeat the same mistake. Ask God to direct you in everything you do. Trust Him. He cares for you. Remember the old saying, "When life gives you lemons, make lemonade." You will find that just about everything that happens to you in your life will have a purpose. It will either be a blessing or a lesson.

Upon You I was cast from birth; You have been my God from my mother's womb. Psalm 22:10 (New American Standard Bible)

The psalmist knew the truth. God had been with him since his birth and even when he was still in his mother's wound. I was blessed with a wonderful mother who loved and trusted God. She took my siblings and me to church every Sunday from a very early age and always lived a good Christian life. I knew about God and His Son, Jesus. I thought I really believed; but truthfully, I think I just took His love for granted until I was a young mother. When I look back, I can see so many times He was there for me. Again, I just took it all for granted. Don't wait as long as I did. What comfort I felt when I truly asked Jesus to come into my heart and promised to give my life to Him.

Today remind yourself that God is there for you and has been since you were born and even before. Seek Him. Trust Him and invite Him into your heart. Life is really so much better, even during the bad times, if you let God hold your hand throughout your life.

"Vanity of vanities," says the Preacher, "Vanity of vanities. All is vanity." Ecclesiastes 1:2 (English Standard Version)

These are the words of King David's son, Solomon, who ruled in Jerusalem. A wonderful story in the Bible tells of Solomon being given a gift from God. He was told he could have anything he wanted and he chose wisdom. Because he asked for wisdom to lead his people and not wealth, God gave him both. He was probably the wealthiest man ever. He had everything he could ever want, yet he was very unhappy. Other versions of this scripture use the word meaningless instead of vanity. Even with all of his power and wealth, Solomon felt life was without meaning or purpose. As for me, all the material things I have had over the years are nothing without my God, my family and my friends. Imagine having only your "things" and no one to love and love you. Even when we feel let down by family and friends, God is always with us showing us the way to cope.

Today notice what you need to be happy. Do all of your many possessions really make your life completely happy? Does that chocolate you crave when you are mad or sad solve the problem? What is missing? Then you might understand how Solomon felt. Do not attempt to fill an emotional hole in your life with money, objects and projects. Nothing or no one can make you completely happy. Only you and you alone can control how you choose to feel. Put emphasis on the right things. The happiest people don't have the best of everything. They just make the best of everything they have. Above all else, accept the love and comfort of Jesus Christ and get to know Him better.

When Jesus spoke again to the people he said, "I am the light of the world. Whoever follows me will never walk in darkness, but will have the light of life." John 8:12 (New International Version)

Rainy and gloomy days certainly can lower your spirits. Some people really become depressed during winter months in states where the weather is so cold and dreary. That is why we love Florida. Even in the sunshine state all days are not sunny, as our life is not always bright. Jesus told us that with Him we will never be gloomy (my words) but will always have a bright spirit in our lives.

Today look for the light in your life. When you feel down-hearted, think of at least one blessing. Dwell on that blessing and find happiness in it. Sometime when I think of so many of my blessings, I get even more discouraged because I feel guilty feeling low when I have so many blessings. There is one blessing that we all have been given… the love of Jesus Christ. That is really all we need to brighten every day of our life. He will always light our path and lead us in the right direction, if we let His sun shine in. My mother used to sing a song to me called, "Let the Sun Shine In" (Face it with a grin. Smilers never lose, and frowners never win. Open up your heart and let the sun shine in.) I sang it to your parents and to the ones of you who would listen. Usually I would get on your nerves singing because I would sing it when you were in a bad mood….not one of my best cheering methods. Wouldn't it be nice if just singing a song could put someone in a happier mood? Singing may not help, but you can always count on the precious love of Jesus to let the sun shine into your heart.

……….eXcept a man be born again, he cannot see the Kingdom of God. John 3:3 (Webster's Bible Translation)

This verse may not exactly start with the letter X, but it is as close as I could get. It is, however, an important verse. What is being born again? Being born again is mentioned many times throughout the New Testament. No, it is not a physical rebirth. It is my opinion and my experience that even though you are raised in a church and believe in Jesus, it is only when you truly accept Him into your life and begin living your life according to His will that you are born again to a new life that is eternal. Yes, there will be many times you will go astray; but we all know Jesus died so we will be forgiven. The Bible also tells us we cannot work our way into heaven by doing good deeds. We only need to "confess with your mouth that Jesus is Lord and believe in your heart that God raised him from the dead, you will be saved." Romans 10:9 (New Living Translation)

Today take time to ask Jesus to come into your heart. Be still and listen. Always be aware that Jesus did not abandon you when He went to heaven. His Holy Spirit will be with you always when you accept Jesus as your Lord and Savior. I have such a peaceful and safe feeling when I remember the Holy Spirit is within me and I am never alone.

You are the salt of the earth, but if salt has lost its taste, how shall its saltiness be restored? It is no longer good for anything except to be thrown out and trampled under people's feet. Matthew 5:13 (English Standard Version)

Salt has many uses, but in the Old Testament it is mostly a purifying agent. Jesus' disciples were to purify a corrupt world through their example and their teaching the Gospel. Jesus knew they would lose their usefulness if they themselves did not set a good example. The same goes for us today. We are called to set a good example for a corrupt world by living a Christian life and encouraging others to want to do the same. Our minister, Dr. Mike Wetzel, made a good point in a sermon once. He said salt is good, but too much salt ruins the food. Sometimes a person who "preaches" too much hurts more than helps. This is not an easy line to walk. I know when I was younger and before I was secure in my relationship with God, I was leery of people who praised God for everything it seemed all the time. Now I have to be aware of my doing this myself and be careful of when I feel I should or should not. I've asked Poppa to call it to my attention when I get too salty.

Today share your love for God with others, but always remember actions speak louder than words. Ask yourself, "What am I teaching through my actions? What do others see in the expressions on my face or hear in the words I speak?" Remember some things are better caught than taught.

Zion will be restored by justice; those who repent will be revived by righteousness. But rebels and sinners will be completely destroyed, and those who desert the LORD will be consumed. Isaiah 1:27-28 (New Living Translation)

Jerusalem is also called Zion, the city of David. Many events in the Bible happened in Zion. It was such an important city that the Lord sent an angel to King David and instructed him to purchase the threshing floor on a mountain near Jerusalem (Mt. Zion) and build an altar where God could be worshiped. Threshing in Biblical times was the harvest-time activity when the grain was removed from the husk and the false grain was separated from the wheat. The process of threshing gave me a visual explanation to this verse, sort of like one of Jesus' parables. After the threshing process, the stalks and grain were thrown up into the air so the wind might blow the unwanted chaff away and leave the valuable kernels. The unwanted chaff would spread over Mt. Zion with no purpose except to die. God will accept those who repent and are useful to his purpose; but the rebels, sinners and deserters will be like the unwanted chaff with no purpose but to be completely destroyed.

Today put yourself in the place of the wheat. Do you want to be heavy with God's love and His word; or do you want to be carefree, doing whatever is pleasing to you and just fly away with no purpose except to come to a useless end? God wants you to fill yourself with thoughts and awareness of His love and become heavy with the Lord's righteousness and grace. "Don't judge each day by the harvest you reap but by the seeds that you plant." Robert Louis Stevenson

Chapter Three

Are any of you suffering hardships? You should pray. Are any of you happy? You should sing praises. James 5:13 (New Living Translation)

Many years ago, I was complaining to my mother about how tired I was of all the problems I seemed to be having. She said, "Oh, Honey. I know lots of people without any problems." When I asked her to name a few she said, "Oh, they're all at the cemetery." She made her point. If you are alive you will have problems and concerns. Do not be discouraged because God cares about you and will help you through any life experience. He will use it for your good and to make your faith stronger. Whenever you do not understand what is going on in your life, just close your eyes, take a deep breath and say, "God, I know it is your plan. Just help me through it, amen" Then believe it. You should always feel free to take everything on your mind to God in prayer. Open your heart to Him and then be still and listen. He may answer with thoughts of how to solve your problem, or He may say, "Wait and trust Me." It is equally important to remember to sing praises to God for all of the happy times with which you have been blessed. Whatever the day looks like from your perspective, whatever season of happiness or sadness you are in today, celebrate God's gift of a new day.

Today pray, not just before you go to sleep but anytime and anywhere. There is no problem too large or too small for God. He doesn't have office hours and is always there for you. Not only will He give you comfort and take away your burdens, you will find true joy when you thank God for your many blessings and are reminded of His precious love.

Be happy with those who are happy, and weep with those who weep. Romans 12:15 (New Living Translation)

This sounds so simple, but I'm afraid it is not always easy to follow. Most of the time it is easy to be happy with a happy person, but what if the reason for the person's happiness is something you had wanted so much for yourself? Sadly, I have known people who are so unhappy themselves that they seem to resent happiness and contentment in others. Of course, we feel sad when someone is suffering. However, there are some people who complain all the time about their health or their life and are never happy. At first it is easy to sympathize, but soon you may find yourself becoming discouraged when hearing it because you know you can do nothing to help. It seems some people enjoy bad health. Sometimes just listening may help. As you all know, my problem is thinking I might have the answer and getting frustrated when my suggestions are ignored. I know I need to listen and not try to solve everything. I promise I'm trying. Poppa says that will take a true miracle.

Today notice how you react to the feelings of others. Do you share their happiness or sadness? Do you really pay attention to their emotions, or do you give a quick "how are you" and go on to something else? How would you feel under the same circumstances? We all feel so much better when someone doesn't just say they care but shows us they care. Let us all try to genuinely "be happy with those who are happy, and weep with those who weep."

Consider the ravens: They do not sow or reap, they have no storeroom or barn; yet God feeds them. And how much more valuable you are than birds! Luke 12:24 (New International Version)

This verse is very important to me. Truthfully, I read Matthew's version first (Matthew 6:28-34), but Luke's version was a good "C" verse. That is another wonderful thing about the Bible. The same story is written by different authors throughout the Bible, and they are all the same or very similar. Have you ever heard of Bible Bingo? It is when you randomly open the Bible and choose a verse or chapter from that page. This is really not the best way to read the Bible, but sometimes I do it when I am searching but do not know for what. One night many years ago, when it seemed as if nothing was going right, I woke up in the middle of the night worrying. I got up, randomly opened my Bible to Matthew 6 and began to read. The section I read was about worrying. I still honestly believe God sent me to that verse. When I read the part about how if God takes care of the birds in the sky and the grass in the fields He would surely take care of me, I felt a peace I had never felt before. I had always gone to church and always believed in God, but that was probably the real beginning of my true faith in my Lord. He is also your Lord. Here is the rest of that story: The next morning I was feeling such peace and knew everything was going to be perfect from then on. Wrong... Lea Ellen and Darren were fussing while getting ready for school. Poppa couldn't find the socks he needed. The peace was gone. When they left, I sat in my favorite chair and cried. I then had a thought from God. He told me that He did not promise life would be without problems, but He would be with me through all times. He certainly has. Trust Him to watch over you. When life has bad turns and you get so discouraged, don't give up. God knows your needs and will provide all you need (not want) in His time.

Today please read Matthew 6. Then play a little Bible Bingo yourself. It's better than any video game, or at least better for you.

Do not be misled: "Bad companionships corrupt good morals." 1 Corinthians 15:33 (New International Version)

Paul wrote these words to the Corinthians. Many members of the church in Corinth were evil and more interested in their own pleasures than living according to God's will. Even good Christians can be tempted by others, and Paul saw this happening in this church. You have heard it said that a rotten apple spoils the whole bunch. This is true in any group, whether it is in our churches or in our group of friends or family. It only takes one person doing what is wrong to tempt others to join in their mischief. Human nature is evil, and we must always remember to stay strong in our beliefs to avoid making mistakes because of the influence of others. It is not wrong for Christians to have friends who do not know God. However, it is very wrong and foolish for a Christian to copy their evil behavior. "Everything you do is based on the choices you make. It's not your parents, your past relationships, your job, the economy, the weather, an argument or your age that is to blame. You and only you are responsible for every decision and every choice you make. Period." (Unknown) Pick your friends wisely. It would be wonderful if you could be a good influence for them; however, if you are being tempted to do evil, walk away. It is inevitable that bad companions will warp our values.

Today think back to the people who have had an influence on your life. Have you been with friends who were doing or saying things you knew in your heart were wrong? Was it easy to tell them no? Were you so anxious to please that you did not use your better judgment in your actions? Strive to be the good influence wherever you are.

Each of you should use whatever gift you have received to serve others, as faithful stewards of God's grace in its various forms. 1 Peter 4:10 (New International Version)

In verse 11 Peter went on to say, "If anyone speaks, they should do so as one who speaks the very words of God. If anyone serves, they should do so with the strength God provides, so that in all things God may be praised through Jesus Christ. To him be the glory and the power for ever and ever." What are your gifts? Yes, I did say gifts. It is true God may have given you a special talent, and you should definitely use that gift. However, I don't believe God wanted us to specialize in only one gift in sharing His love with others. Sometimes I find myself thinking I need to do something really special and end up doing nothing at all. Often just a smile, a phone call or a card can mean so much to someone just needing to know someone cares. Use your special talent, but always be alert to any needs of those around you. Helping others individually or working with organizations are equally important. John Wesley, founder of the Methodist Church, said: "Do all the good you can, by all the means you can, in all the ways you can, in all the places you can, at all the times you can, to all the people you can, as long as ever you can." That is a lot of "can's", but the world is filled with "can's" that need to be done. Do your share, always giving God the glory.

Today ask yourself, "What are my special talents? How can I use them to help others?" I know each of you has the special talent of making me happy when we are together by your just taking time to smile at me and stop to visit a few minutes. When we are apart I get so excited when I get an email or a call from you. Does someone need help with a chore? Mothers always need help. Notice how good it feels when someone helps you, and don't forget to thank God and give Him the glory for your gifts and the gifts of others.

For God didn't give us a spirit of fear, but of power, love, and self-control. 2 Timothy 1:7 (New Living Translation)

This is a verse I definitely need to remember daily. I'm always finding myself fearful something will happen to my family. I'm always a little afraid of new experiences, especially if I am to meet new people. It may be silly, but one of my greatest fears is I am going to say something stupid or hurtful unintentionally. Maybe because I usually do. The spirit of fear was given to me by myself. God wants me to use the important spirits He has given me. I need to use His power, love and self-control to give me confidence to handle anything life sends my way. I need to appreciate and enjoy the new experiences and the new people I meet. If I use self-control and think before I speak, I won't need to fear misspeaking. Does fear ever stop you from doing things you really would like to do?

Today face your fears. Remember this verse and think of it every time you find yourself apprehensive. Remember the spirit of power, love and self-control God has given you. Trust Him and do not waste your day being insecure. Live your life looking forward to each day with confidence. "A ship in harbor is safe, but that is not what ships are built for." John A. Shedd. God built us with the spirits needed to live the wonderful life He has given us to the fullest, not to "stay safe in the harbor" with the spirit of fear.

Success is never final. Failure is never fatal. It is courage that counts." Winston Churchill

"Our greatest glory is not in never failing, but in rising up every time we fail." Ralph Waldo Emerson

"A person who never made a mistake never tried anything new." Albert Einstein (and Poppa repeats all the time.)

Gracious words are a honeycomb, sweet to the soul and healing to the bones. Proverbs 16:24 (New International Version)

It doesn't even have to be gracious words to make me feel so good inside. I love it when I say something and Poppa really laughs. It makes me feel like I made him happy. Just a cheerful attitude adds so much to everyone's life. Of course, if someone is really sad, soothing words or just listening is probably the best medicine. On the other hand, I feel very sad and upset when someone says something hateful to me or just gives me a look of anger. In one of Dr. Mike Wetzel's sermons he told us one of the biggest mistakes we make is believing there is a tomorrow. We never know what will happen, and we should live each day as if it is our last. Isn't it scary to know any time could be the last time you talk to anyone? Keep that in mind. I certainly pray my last words or the last words someone else hears from me will be gracious words. I can assure this by using only words pleasing to God.

Today pay attention to your words. Are they sweet and do they add to the happiness of those around you? Or are they too harsh and hurtful? Notice how others speak to you. Sometimes the hateful ones may be unhappy themselves, and you could make them a little sweeter by kind words. Other times you may just need to hold your tongue and ignore. My mother always told me, "If you can't say anything nice, don't say anything at all." Pretty good advice.

He will wipe every tear from their eyes, and there will be no more death or sorrow or crying or pain. All these things are gone forever. Revelation 21:4 (New International Version)

The book of Revelation is a difficult book to read and understand, or at least for me. Poppa is summarizing it for you, and I can't wait to read it. Heaven is described in Revelation. No one really knows exactly how it will be in Heaven. There are stories told of people who have had near-death experiences and described what they saw. The Bible tells us what a wonderful place it will be. I love this verse. Imagine never having anything to cause pain again. We will not have to lose those we love again, because there is no death in Heaven. When I think of Heaven I get excited. It sounds wonderful. I don't know if it is right or wrong; but as much as I look forward to Heaven, I thank God every day for the extra time He has given me with you. As young as you are, I would imagine it would be hard to get excited about going to Heaven right now. Appreciate every moment you have been given. "Sometimes you will never know the value of a moment until it becomes a memory." …. Dr. Suess. Poppa and I did not really appreciate so many things while we were young that we would certainly appreciate now, especially our health. We now know the meaning of the old saying, "Youth is wasted on the young."

Today thank God for your gift of another day and live it in a way pleasing to God. The great thing about getting to Heaven is you don't have to work your way there. All you have to do is accept Jesus as God's Son and your Savior. If you do this, living a way pleasing to Jesus will be a joy, not a chore. "For grace is given not because we have done good works, but in order that we may be able to do them". St. Augustine

I can do all things through Christ, who strengthens me. Philippians 4:13 (World English Bible)

On October 10, 2010, I awoke with a very strange pain in the top of my mouth. I am not one to panic, but for some reason I knew I needed to have it checked. I honestly believe God was guiding me. I awakened Poppa and told him I needed to go to the emergency room. The rest is history with a good ending. I had a dissected aorta, which is usually fatal. I was in a coma for almost a month. This was a horrible time for Poppa and your parents. While in the coma, I can remember many times being so scared and fighting to get up. I can still see and feel the crowd I felt was holding me down. When this happened there would be an opening in the crowd. I didn't see anyone; but I could hear in my heart the words of this verse, "I can do all things through Christ who strengthens me", and I would feel a wonderful peace. It is my theme verse every day of my life, and I pray it will be yours. Your life is just beginning. I know you have already had more than your share of problems. Most of them are over, some are not. There will be other trials, because that is a part of life. "Life is not meant to be easy. It is meant to be LIVED; sometimes happy, sometimes rough…. but with ups and downs that make you STRONG." Charlie Brown (Charles Schultz). Just remember you will survive all trials because of the love and strength you receive from our Savior, Jesus Christ.

Today think about this verse. Christ gave you strength in the past, whether you realized it or not; and I promise He will always give you strength in the future. Remember this verse in everything you do today and always. Not only will it give you strength; hopefully it will also remind you not to waste a day in your life. God and the wonderful doctors gave me more time with Poppa, your parents and you. Now Poppa and I do not take one day for granted. You do the same, and have a great life doing all things through Christ who gives you strength.

Jesus said to His disciples: "Things that cause people to stumble are bound to come, but woe to anyone through whom they come." Luke 17:1 (New International Version)

Considering human nature and the evil temptations all around us, it is no wonder we experience stumbling blocks in our lives. Jesus knew this would be so. Some of the commentaries I have read about this verse say to stumble could mean to doubt their faith or to tempt to sin. I have heard it jokingly said that if you want to lose your religion, become active in a church. Just yesterday Poppa took something by our church and was met by one of the ladies of the church with an attitude that tempted Poppa to have unreligious thoughts. This is a small example of the lesson I feel Jesus is teaching. As His disciples, it is our responsibility to show God's love to all around and give encouragement rather than tempt them to "lose their religion". Have you ever noticed that the ones in a crowd who are doing something wrong are always trying to get others to join them? I guess they don't feel as guilty if others are doing it too. Don't be one of these people. Live a life encouraging other to live a good life, not tempting them to sin. We are to help remove the stumbling blocks so all can see the road Jesus wants us to take. Don't make the stack larger by tempting others to stumble.

Today be aware of your actions. Do you influence others to live a life pleasing to Jesus? Always remember Jesus' warning and never be the one who influences others to sin. One of our main purposes in life is to help others; and if you can't help them, at least don't hurt them.

Keep yourselves in God's love as you wait for the mercy of our Lord Jesus Christ to bring you to eternal life. Jude 1:21 (New International Version)

I have done it again. I have spent too much time studying this verse to make it interesting for you. Some of the commentaries were written in the 1800's and I didn't really understand a word they said. Yes, many times other resources are definitely needed to give you a better understanding of the words in the Bible. However, when I read the words as written in God's Holy Bible again.... Duh! It says it all. I know it is true. If you keep yourself aware of the love of God, which is always with you, looking for the mercy of our Lord Jesus Christ for eternal life will be a natural joy. Some verses can also stand alone to give you encouragement and peace of mind. As you keep yourselves in the love of God, also keep yourselves in the Word of God.

Today "Keep yourselves in God's love as you wait for the mercy of our Lord Jesus Christ to bring you to eternal life." Be aware of the peaceful feeling inside you when you truly accept God's love will never fail. He loves you no matter what you do or do not do. I know I have talked a lot about heaven in this book. Some people have doubts about heaven. The Bible makes it very clear that Jesus has gone to prepare a place for us. No, we cannot check out pictures of heaven on the computer. We must again have faith of what we cannot see. I love believing someday we will all be together forever in heaven. I love the relationship I have with our God and His Son, and I pray you will have that relationship also. Heaven is real to me. Yes, I will keep myself in the love of God until He takes me to eternal life.

Likewise, the tongue is a small part of the body, but it makes great boasts. Consider what a great forest is set on fire by a small spark. James 3:5 (New International Version)

Our family loves to talk. The tongue has given us many happy times of great conversations. It has also given us times of consoling each other during times of sadness. As helpful as this small part of our body is, we all know how powerful it can be. I still remember the hurt I felt when I was in the first or second grade and a girl told me her mother didn't want her to play with me. I found out later her mother had not said that. She just wanted to hurt me, and she certainly did. I also remember the sweet words of the nurse who helped me and comforted me when I was in the hospital to have my first baby and was so afraid. Both of these incidents happened many years ago; however, I still remember both incidents as if they were yesterday. Does your tongue set a fire of joy, or do you destroy the spirits of others by your sharp words?

Today watch not only your words but also the tone of your voice and the expression on your face. Remember your tongue may be a small spark, but it is a powerful flame. Will people remember the hurt you caused or the happiness spread by your words?

Make sure that nobody pays back wrong for wrong, but always strive to do what is good for each other and for everyone else. 1 Thessalonians 5:15 (New International Version)

This is definitely not the only verse in the Bible giving this advice. We are told over and over again that revenge is prohibited in the life of a Christian. We are to wait for the Lord. He has told us He will handle it and He will. Remember the Golden Rule? "Therefore, whatever you want others to do for you, do also the same for them--this is the Law and the Prophets." Matthew 7:12 (Holman Christian Standard Bible) It didn't say we should do unto others as they do unto us. We are to love our enemies and pray for those who persecute us. This is one of the hardest things we are asked to do, but it is one of the most important acts we can do to give us peace in our lives. Some people make this so difficult for us and seem to continue to be a thorn in our side. Life becomes easier when we learn to accept the apology we may never get, knowing vengeance is the Lord's.

Today do not pay back wrong with wrong. If someone says or does something hurtful to you, do not be hurtful back to them. I would think eventually anyone would get tired of not getting a reaction to their evil acts. Remember what your Grandmomma has always told you. "Two wrongs do not make a right."

Now faith is being sure of what we hope for, being convinced of what we do not see. Hebrews 11:1 (NET Bible)

I have never seen the wind, but I have seen the movement of objects caused by the wind. I have also felt the wind against my face and in my hair. No, I cannot see God; but I have felt His presence and His reassurance so many times in my life. I have seen the results of God's care in my life and in the life of those around me. I also feel God's presence in the beautiful world He has given us. We are told in the Bible we are to live by faith and not by sight. We are shown throughout the Bible the steps of faith taken by our forefathers, preparing the way and setting examples for our faith today. Faith is a gift from God, but we must nurture our faith to keep it strong. Faith is like a muscle. If exercised, it grows strong. If left immobile, it becomes weak. We grow in our faith by getting to know God through prayer and studying the Bible.

Today read Hebrew 11. The examples and testimonies of the faith of the men and women we read about in this chapter show us we too can live by faith.

Out of the mouth of babies and infants, you have established strength because of your foes, to still the enemy and the avenger. Psalm 8:2 (English Standard Version)

I know you have heard many times that children should be seen but not heard. Jesus did not feel that way. He loved the enthusiasm and innocence of little children. He wanted all of us to have the faith a child has before being influenced by the sometimes-cruel world. Jesus made it clear that children were welcomed and loved by Him. Once Jesus cleared the temple of money-changers because they had "turned the temple from a house of worship into a den of thieves." He remained in the temple and began healing the blind and the lame. The head priests and scribes saw these wonderful miracles and heard the praises from all the people. They were upset the children were also praising Jesus. They wanted the children cleared from the temple. Jesus then quoted the above verse from Psalm. (Matthew 21:16). Jesus appreciated the praise from the children. Don't ever lose your childish faith. You could be the one who influences others to love Jesus and live according to His word.

Today be aware of what comes "out of your mouth of babies". Are you letting doubts of the world come into your heart, or do you still believe as you did when you were very young? Instead of being influenced by the world, let your light shine so others can see your love of Jesus and your faith of a child. Stop the enemies and avengers who want to "turn your life of worship into a den of thieves," stealing your faith.

Peter replied, "Man, I don't know what you're talking about!" Just as he was speaking, the rooster crowed. The Lord turned and looked straight at Peter. Then Peter remembered the word the Lord had spoken to him: "Before the rooster crows today, you will disown me three times." And he went outside and wept bitterly. Luke 22:60-62 (New International Version)

Have you, like Peter, ever denied Jesus? If you don't remember this story you can read it in the 22nd chapter of Luke. It wasn't easy for me to share my faith and love for God and His Son when I was younger. I hesitated to even talk about God or Jesus for fear others would think I was too judgmental and felt I was better than they were. Today I freely talk about what God has done and continues to do in my life. I think in other ways I still deny, ignore, or forget to allow God/Jesus into my life. It is not that God has moved away from me, it is because I have allowed other things to get in the way of my relationship with God. Too often I give into negative feelings and emphasize the bad rather than remember the joy I have when I let Jesus into my heart. I also still worry and forget to turn to God/Jesus for comfort and help. When looking back on my life I realize my hardest times often led to the greatest moments of my life. We all need to keep the faith, as it will be worth it in the end.

Today do not deny Jesus. Share your love for Him with others. Also, do not deny His love and His blessings in your life. Every time you feel negative or worried about a situation, do not deny Jesus' help and comfort. Listen to Jesus not Satan. I would much rather deny Satan. What about you?

You may have noticed that I randomly use God and Jesus. This is again when the Trinity is difficult for me to completely understand. In this incident, I think of God and Jesus as the same. However, sometimes I pray to God, consider Jesus His Son and an example of how we should live. I do accept the Holy Trinity, the Father, Son and Holy Spirit. I just seem to have trouble when writing. That's okay. God knows what I mean. I hope you do too.

Quench not the Spirit. Despise not prophesyings. Prove all things; hold fast that which is good. Abstain from all appearance of evil. 1 Thessalonians 5:19-22 (King James Bible)

In this letter Paul is advising the church members and especially their leaders to be ready when Jesus returns. He knew there would be different opinions in the church, as there still are today. Just because someone thinks differently than we do does not mean we should not listen. However, we do need to always hold onto the teachings of the Bible and keep the flame of the Spirit burning in our lives. Today there are so many ways of life accepted. Just because it is accepted by society does not mean it is the right thing to do. I honestly believe if we hold on to the good and avoid what we know is wrong, not only will we be ready when Jesus returns, but we will have a life filled with more contentment than regrets.

Today notice if you are doing something you know is wrong but you have seen on television so often it seems as if it is okay. How would you feel if you knew Jesus had you on Skype? We seem to be on cameras wherever we go. Would you be proud to see your actions on U-tube? Don't quench that wonderful flame burning in your life.

***Return to your rest, my soul, for the LORD has been good to you.
Psalm 116:7 (New International Version)***

Poppa and I have been blessed with a wonderful life and many wonderful memories. However, we have had what some might say more than our share of difficult and stressful times. It was during these hard times I really began to feel God's presence in my life. When I look back, it is as if God was preparing us for these times. We were working with the youth of our church during the first really hard times, and we received so much support from them. We later moved to Florida because of Poppa's health and were in the right place near doctors who could literally save my life when I had a dissected aorta. I will forever be grateful to Dr. Michael DeFrain, a cardiothoracic surgeon, and Dr. Mohamed Ali, a pulmonologist, who gave me such special care and helped, not only me but your Poppa and parents, through a very stressful and scary time in our lives. Years later, Poppa was blessed to received excellent treatment and was saved when he had to have Whipple surgery to remove cancer from his pancreas. He has had so many health problem, including a saddle blood clot in both lungs, and the doctors in Florida have been great. The list goes on and on. The older I get the easier it is to find God's comfort early in a bad situation, but I still have trouble turning to God in less serious problems. The Lord will give rest to our soul even in everyday situations. He is with us every minute of the day and night, helping us as well as blessing us.

Today when something upsets you or causes you unhappiness, stop immediately and remember this verse. Think of the many times God has blessed you. Then ask Him to help you find rest from your worry, anger or hurt. Spend the rest of your time appreciating how good God has been to you and how He has been and will forever be there for you.

So, when they continued asking Him, He lifted up himself, and said unto them, "He that is without sin among you, let him first cast a stone at her." John 8:7 (King James Bible)

The teachers of the law and the Pharisees had brought a woman, who had been caught in adultery, to Jesus and asked Him what they should do. They made her stand before the group and said to Jesus, "In the Law Moses commanded us to stone such women. Now what do you say?" They were using this question as a trap in order to have a basis for accusing Jesus. Jesus bent down and started to write on the ground with his finger. When they kept on questioning him, he straightened up and answered with your verse for today. I love His answer. He said anyone who had not sinned should throw the first stone. Everyone left. Jesus then told the woman to go and sin no more. Could you have thrown that first stone?

Today when you start to criticize someone or tell of something they have done wrong, stop and think if you are free of any wrong yourself. My granny and mother always told me, "There is so much good in the worst of us and so much bad in the best of us, that it hardly behooves any of us to talk about the rest of us." Jesus knew we all are sinners. He gave His life so our sins will be forgiven. Now try to follow His advice and "Go and sin no more."

The heavens declare the glory of God; the skies proclaim the work of his hands. Psalm 19:1 (New International Version)

When I was a child I would lie on a blanket, looking at the clouds and imagining different things they resembled. Later in my life I did the same with my children and with some of my grandchildren. I always felt so close to God at this time and felt the work of His hands. After reading, "The clouds are the dust of His feet," (Nahum 1:3 NIV) I now look at the sky realizing how big our God is. Poppa and I never tire of sunrises and sunsets. We have so many pictures. Living in Florida, we have some days when there is not a cloud in the sky. How can anyone look at the heavens and the beauty of all nature and not feel the glory of God? It is true we cannot see God and some people claim the world just happened, but "faith is being convinced of what we cannot see" (Hebrews 11:1 NET). I can see God's nature, and I am certain He made it; and "It is very good." (Genesis 1:31 NIV).

Today look up, not just as the heavens but at your Heavenly Father. Too often we take the world around us for granted. See the glory of God around you and call it to the attention to others. Don't forget to send up to Heaven a great big "Thank You"

Use hospitality one to another without grumbling. 1 Peter 4:9 (King James Bible)

As I write this devotion, the time could not be more appropriate. Poppa and I just returned from a cruise with six of our closest friends. We all were celebrating our 50th and 53rd wedding anniversaries. We had a wonderful time but are completely exhausted. Everyone came back to our house for a few days and just left this morning. It would have been so easy to grumble, and I probably would have if I had not felt so blessed. Great friends. We were all so happy to be able to be together one more time. This is not always true of other situations and I have to work hard at not grumbling. It is all in the attitude.

Today if someone interrupts your activity make an effort to make them feel welcomed. Stop and visit. Listen to what they have to say. You can put down your video game for a few minutes to show your hospitality without grumbling. Try it. You might enjoy it. One thing for certain, you will add joy to the life of someone else.

Very truly I tell you, the one who believes has eternal life.
John 6:47 (New International Version)

Jesus spoke these words after not only feeding at least five thousand people with five small barley loaves and two small fish, but also walking on water to his disciples' boat. Read John 6 for a great story and explanation. Jesus told all of these followers that He alone had seen God and the only way they would someday see God was to believe Jesus was His Son. When you think about it, how could you believe in God and not believe He sent His Son to us to show us the way? He had tried everything to get our attention; but it was only after He sent His Son to die for us, and then be resurrected, that we really knew God had given us the hope of an everlasting life.

Today think about Jesus. Think about what you have learned about Him. Sing a song about Jesus. Most people know "Jesus Loves Me". You might want to reverse the words to "Jesus knows me this I love". He knows everything about you and still loves you. He is waiting for you to ask Him into your heart. Do it today. He will walk beside you now and FOREVER.

***Wanting to satisfy the crowd, Pilate released Barabbas to them. He had Jesus flogged and then handed Him over to them to crucify.* Mark 15:15 (New International Version)**

Pilate did not release Barabbas instead of Jesus because Jesus had done anything wrong. He released this murderer because he wanted to please the crowd. Are you ever tempted to go against your better judgment to please others? We deal with people we want to please all the time. Your "crowd" might be friends at school, or the "crowd" could be just one person to whom you find it hard to say no. Too often we give in and do things we know are wrong or treat others in a hurtful way because "everyone else is doing it" and we don't want to go against the crowd. As you mature, you realize it is less important to have lots of friends and more important to have real ones with the same morals and interests as you.

Today think about times in the past when you have gone along with the "crowd" even though you knew it was wrong. The next time you are in a crowd that wants to do something you know is wrong, ask yourself: Are you choosing Barabbas or Jesus?

eXalt the LORD our God and worship at His footstool; Holy is He. Psalm 99:5 (New International Version)

A footstool is a piece of furniture that sits in front of an "easy chair". When I think of your Papaw (Poppa's dad) I always can see him in his easy chair with his feet on the footstool. When Poppa wanted a serious discussion with him, he would sometimes sit on that stool. Lea Ellen and Darren loved to talk to Papaw while sitting on the stool and eventually would work their way up into his lap. We are told by this verse in Psalm to come to a "footstool" before God and exalt Him. To exalt is to hold or raise someone up to a high position or status. Yes, we all looked up to Papaw as someone special; but no one or nothing is more special than our God. God loves us and wants us to feel free to sit on His footstool in a child-like way and have a special and private time with Him. What an honor and privilege we are given to receive such a special invitation from the most exalted.

Today find a footstool. Place it in front of a chair. If you can't find a stool just sit on the floor. Then pretend God is sitting in that chair. "Talk" to the chair as if God were sitting in it. You can share any feeling you have with God. You may not be able to see Him, but He will hear your every word. You are His child and He will take you into His arms and put you on His lap. Feel His love.

You are the light of the world. A town built on a hill cannot be hidden. Neither do people light a lamp and put it under a bowl. Instead they put it on its stand, and it gives light to everyone in the house. In the same way, let your light shine before others, that they may see your good deeds and glorify your Father in heaven. Matthew 5:14-16 (New International Version)

Matthew 5 is the introduction to Jesus' famous Sermon on the Mount. Jesus is lighting the lamp of the everlasting Gospel and encouraging others to spread His Word. Because His disciples did as He asked, we are given His wonderful words of comfort in times of need and guidance on how we should live. We are not to fear shining the light of our love for Jesus "so others will see our good deeds and glorify our Father in Heaven." Have you ever known someone whose presence lights up a room? What about someone who brings only gloom and doom to a group. Which one do you enjoy being with the most? Which are you? When you love God and trust Him in your life, you will feel the peace and contentment His love supplies. You then will find it easy to let your light shine before others and live in a way others will see your love for God and want to find that same joy. Even the best Christians have bad days, but they also have faith God will help in every situation. God will relight your lamp as many times as you ask. His power is forever. Our world is in great need of the light of Jesus' love. Jesus tells us we are the light of the world. Shine your light. Never be the one to bring a dark cloud over others.

Today notice the people with whom you come in contact. Who is happy? Who is negative and gloomy? How do they make you feel? How about you? Are you shining a light of happiness and encouragement, or are you acting in a way to snuff the light of others? You may think that your actions don't really have much effect on others. Not true. I know when I am around you and you are happy I am overjoyed. However, I am so discouraged and sad when you are in a negative and bad mood. I love you as God does, no matter what your mood; but I pray you will let the beautiful light of your love shine for others and for me.

Zedekiah was 21 years old when he became king, and he reigned eleven years in Jerusalem. Jeremiah 52:1 (New International Version)

Zedekiah was just one of many kings mentioned in the scriptures. Poppa is writing in his book so much information about all of the kings. Of course, I chose this king because of "Z". As it is today, there were some good and some bad kings or leaders. The people were very much affected by the type of leadership; and the countries, of course, benefited more from the good and faithful leaders who led according to God's will. What type of leader would you be? I would like to think I would follow the teachings of God and do only what is best for the people. It seems too often leaders did, and still do, become so involved with their own power, prestige and possession they ignore the needs of the country and the normal citizens. It is never too early to start paying attention to the local, state and national elected officials, and when you are old enough remember to vote. Who knows? Someday one of you might become President of the United States. Anything is possible.

Today think about the "kings" you have had in your life. No, not real kings but people who have ruled over you, such as your teachers, coaches and, of course your parents and grandparents. How did they make you feel? Remember sometimes it may seem they are not doing it for your own good, but you may realize later that they were. When Poppa and I were in high school we had a principal, Mr. W. D. Human, whom everyone really feared. We realize now that he was just what our school needed and we wish there were more Mr. Humans in our schools today. When you are given the opportunity to be the leader of a group, will you be the leader the group wants, or the leader the group needs? When you lead following God's will you cannot go wrong.

Chapter Four

And we know that all things work together for good for those who love God, who are called according to his purpose. Romans 8:28 (New International Version)

I have always heard it said everything happens for a reason. That is not to say God makes bad things happen to us to fulfill His plan. Accidents happen. Health problems occur. People hurt us. We make mistakes which cause problems. God does, however, help us make it through all our problems if we only trust Him. It is with His guidance and the lessons we learn from the experience, both good and bad, that we see how God does work it all for good according to the plan He has for our lives. When I look back on my life, I can honestly say it is hard to find any problem which did not make me stronger or serve a purpose in my life. Sometimes God lets you hit rock bottom so you will discover He is the solid rock at the bottom. With His help, you will find the strength to make it back to the top. Have patience, remembering patience is not only the ability to wait but also the ability to keep a good attitude while waiting.

Today when anything goes wrong, try to look for the good in that situation. As you get older you will find this easier to do. If you put your faith in God and strive to survive the situation, rather than let it defeat you, you will look back some day on so many experiences in your life and truly see how your life is better and you are a stronger Christian because you survived. You will also realize the lessons learned and the good things which happened because of them. On the next page is a cute story about not giving up. I love the moral of the story. God even uses donkeys as examples for us.

The Donkey Story

One day a farmer's donkey fell down into a well. The animal cried pitifully for hours as the farmer tried to figure out what to do. Finally, he decided the animal was old and the well needed to be covered up anyway; it just wasn't worth it to retrieve the donkey. He invited all his neighbors to come over and help him. They all grabbed a shovel and began to shovel dirt into the well. At first, the donkey realized what was happening and cried horribly. Then, to everyone's amazement he quieted down.

A few shovel loads later, the farmer finally looked down the well. He was astonished at what he saw. With each shovel of dirt that hit his back, the donkey was doing something amazing. He would shake it off and take a step up. As the farmer's neighbors continued to shovel dirt on top of the animal, he would shake it off and take a step up. Pretty soon, everyone was amazed as the donkey stepped up and over the edge of the well and happily trotted off.

MORAL

Life is going to shovel dirt on you, all kinds of dirt. The trick to getting out of the well is to shake it off and take a step up. Each of our troubles is a steppingstone. We can get out of the deepest wells just by not stopping, never giving up! Shake it off and take a step up.

Don't forget the best stepping stone is faith in God to show the way.

Brothers and sisters, I do not consider myself yet to have taken hold of it. But one thing I do: Forgetting what is behind and straining toward what is ahead, I press on toward the goal to win the prize for which God has called me Heavenward in Christ Jesus. Philippians 3:13-14 (New International Version)

This verse was written by the Apostle Paul. If anyone ever had a past he would want to forget, it would be Paul. Read about him in Acts 9. Paul was named Saul until Jesus spoke to him on the Road to Damascus and changed him from being the chief persecutor of followers of Jesus Christ to the leader who would establish Christianity as we know it today. Even though Paul wrote thirteen books in the New Testament, he still did not feel he had all the answers. So, don't feel bad if you feel the same. Paul knew he just needed to look toward each day with hope and faith. We all have memories in our past which cause us unhappiness. Maybe someone hurt us or we hurt someone. If God could forgive Paul, we know He has forgiven all involved in our past, including us. We should also be able to forgive. God doesn't want us to waste another day in the life He has given us by dwelling on the past. One of the happiest moments ever is when you find the courage to let go of what you cannot change. We definitely cannot change the past, but we can change how we let it affect our future.

Today notice every time you remember or remind someone of something done in the past that bothered you. When this happens, think of something good they have done which pleased you. "When one door closes, another one opens; but we often look so long and so regretfully upon the closed door that we do not see the one which opens for us." ----Alexander Graham Bell. We must strive for progress, not perfection. We will never be perfect on this earth, but we should never stop pressing on toward the prize God has promised us in Jesus Christ.

Can any of you add a single hour to the length of your life by worrying? Matthew 6:27 (International Standard Version)

How can I, of all people, give you advice on worrying? I can honestly tell you that worrying has not added an hour to my life but has taken so many hours away. I have wasted many precious days and even ruined my health by worrying. I have always considered myself a person of faith, but my worrying tells me I didn't have enough. I have finally realized that if I leave everything in God's hand I will eventually see God's hand in everything. All of my worrying did not make one thing happen or not happen. In fact, I see that most of the things I worried about didn't even happen. I also see how God has used the ones that did happen for a reason. It is still my tendency to start to worry. When this happens I immediately seek God. He is my strength and continues to help me through every situation.

Just for today think about what is causing you to worry. Is there anything you can do about it? If so, do it. If not, think of the many times you have worried about something that did not happen. Then look for the good in your life and enjoy what you have. With God's help, your worries of today will pass. Remember today will never happen again. Try not to let your worries keep you from enjoying this day that God has given you. Give your worries to God. He is in control anyway.

Do not let anyone look down on you because you are young, but set an example for the believers in speech, in conduct, in love, in faith and in purity. 1 Timothy 4:12 (New International Version)

You are never too young to set a good example for others. In Mark 10:15 (NIV) Jesus said, "Truly I tell you, anyone who will not receive the kingdom of God like a little child will never enter it." Children are so trusting and sincere in their beliefs. It is the adults who teach them to doubt and be prejudice and judgmental. It was the example set by a high school football teammate of Darren's that helped me when I was in a coma from a dissected aorta. This young man wore a towel on his football uniform that said, "I can do all things through Christ who gives me strength." Philippians 4:13 (Berean Study Bible). I remembered this verse because of him, and it was what I kept thinking of when I wasn't even expected to live. I was given strength through Christ and was aware of it because this teammate and friend of Darren's, who at a young age when he could have been teased for showing his faith, had the courage to share his faith and put that verse on my heart. I would love to put this young man's name in my book, but I cannot do it without his permission. Another lesson has been taught by this same person. Stay in touch with your friends! Even with Facebook and all other technology available now, my son and I were unable to locate this special young man who had moved away from our area because of employment. Don't let this happen to you.

Today ask yourself, "What am I teaching through my actions? What do others see in the expressions on my face or hear in my words?" Do not lose your innocence of youth. Be aware of times you give into negative thoughts and actions. Are you setting a good example for those around you who may have become so wrapped up in life's problems they have forgotten to have faith?

Every good and perfect gift is from above, coming down from the Father of the heavenly lights, who does not change like shifting shadows. James 1:17 (New International Version)

"The best things in life are free." The older I get the more I realize the truth of this statement. Just look around you. We have the sun, moon, stars, sky, clouds, rain, mountains, oceans, family, friends...and the list goes on and on. The best free gift we could ever be given is the love of our Heavenly Father. He was the same yesterday as He is today and will always be. Yes, God's love is a gift that will always be the same and will never be broken. He has promised us the free gift of life everlasting. His Son, Jesus, paid the price for us with His death on the cross. Accept that gift and cherish it.

Today look around you. Count all your gifts from above, and do not forget to thank God for all your blessings. Remember, it is true. The best gifts in life are free

For I know the plans I have for you, declares the Lord, plans for welfare and not for evil, to give you a future and a hope. Jeremiah 29:11 (New American Standard 1977)

God sent this message through His prophet Jeremiah to the remainder of His people, who had been held captive for seventy years in Babylon. He wanted them to know He had not forgotten them and to give them hope for the future. God's message is the same for us today. With God, there is always hope. You are now at an age when you feel a need to know what you want to do with your life. I am now at an age when I have lived most of the life you are planning. It is such a good feeling to know God isn't finished with either of us yet. As you plan your life's work, always remember God will be with you. He has a very good plan for your life. Seek His guidance. You may not see it immediately and may even change your directions many times. Don't waste your life worrying about what will or should happen. Enjoy each day as it comes. God doesn't want us to just sit around waiting for Him to tell us what to do. Be alert to all opportunities that come your way. Do everything to be prepared when the right one comes along. Remember as you add years to your life, add life to your years. Most importantly, go to God in prayer. Don't just talk. Listen.

Today live for this day only. There is nothing wrong with preparing for the future. In fact, it is the wise thing to do. However, each day do the best you can on what needs to be done and trust God for tomorrow.

Four Things You Can't Recover

The STONE after the throw.
The WORD after it is said.
The OCCASION after it is missed.
The TIME after it is gone

Deanna Wadsworth

***Get rid of all bitterness, rage and anger, brawling and slander, along with every form of malice. Be kind and compassionate to one another, forgiving each other just as in Christ God forgave you.*
Ephesians 4:31-32 (New International Version)**

Bitterness, rage and anger come way too easy. We know in our heart it is wrong. We love Jesus and want to be like Him. We even know how much better our life is when we follow the advice of these verses. Then why is it so hard? Human nature seems to be naturally evil. The truth is, once you are aware of these feelings in your heart and consciously work at removing them, it becomes easier and easier. I don't think it is possible to have a great relationship with everyone, but we do need to always be kind and considerate of others. Jesus died on the cross so our sins would be forgiven. As He was dying, Jesus said, "Father, forgive them, for they do not know what they are doing." (Luke 23:34 NIV). We also should ask God to help us forgive those who have caused us to become bitter and angry. They too may not know what they have done. If they are aware, then they especially need our prayers for them to become more loving people. Do not regret knowing the people who come into your life. Good people give you happiness. Bad ones give you experience. The worst ones give you lessons. The best people give you good memories.

Today be aware of every time you remember something that causes you to become bitter. Notice when you are angry and argumentative or have any other form of evil thoughts or actions. Also, be aware of the times you are kind and compassionate to someone and when you are able to forgive someone as God has forgiven you. Which feels right and makes you happiest? Okay, I'll be honest. I can just hear a few of you saying, "I feel better when I can get even." That really makes me sad. There is no peace in revenge, only more conflicts. Forgiveness doesn't make the other person right. It makes you free to live in peace, knowing you are doing God's will.

He gives strength to the weary and strengthens the powerless. Isaiah 40:29 (Holman Christian Standard Bible)

He sure does!!!!!! I alone am not a very strong or confident person; but with God I find the strength I need in all situations, serious or minor. God gave me strength to recover from my near-death experience with a dissected aorta. He also has given me needed strength to just make it through a really stressful day. This book would never end if I wrote all the times I have felt God's strength inside of me. I hate to admit it, but when I was younger I didn't always reach out to life as I wish I had. I was always afraid of failure. Someone once told me failure is something we can avoid by saying nothing, doing nothing and being nothing. This is not the life I want. I am so grateful I was able to accept the strength God offered me. I have also heard it said, "When God pushes you to the edge trust Him full because only two things can happen. Either He will catch you when you fall or He will teach you how to fly." Because of my faith in God and the encouragement of the wonderful man He gave me (your Poppa), life has taken me places and given me more opportunities than I feel I deserve. It is wonderful to know the best is yet to come.

Today if there is anything causing you doubt or concern, ask God to give you strength and courage. Then do it. Feel Him beside you all the way. Now that wasn't bad, was it? With this attitude and trust in God, you will never have to look back and wish you had taken a chance. "If you learn from defeat, you haven't really lost." Zig Ziglar ….. Yes, the best is yet to come.

In the same way, the Spirit helps us in our weakness. We do not know what we ought to pray for, but the Spirit himself intercedes for us through wordless groans. Romans 8:26 (New International Version)

When we accept Jesus into our heart, we receive the Holy Spirit He promised so we will never be alone. The Trinity (Three in one… Father, Son and Holy Spirit) is sometimes confusing to me. I always pray to God, our Father. I try to live by the examples of Jesus, His Son, and sometimes I "talk" to Jesus also. The Holy Spirit is so important but sometimes I forget. When I stop to realize the Holy Spirit is right here within me, it is such an amazing feeling. But I also feel God and Jesus are with me always…. thus, the three in one. According to this verse, sometimes we have trouble finding the right words to tell God what is on our heart, or we may not even be sure how we feel or what we should want. Don't worry. The Holy Spirit will do our praying for us; and if we listen, we will know the answer. Sometimes you may have to wait on the answer, but you can be certain that God is at work in your life. What a wonderful feeling to know the Father, Son and Holy Spirit are with you always. I don't have to understand it. I just have to accept it, and I do.

Today be aware the Holy Spirit is within you. Any time during the day when you feel happy, sad, confused, mad and all of the other emotions we have, be aware Your Holy Spirit is right there, knows your feelings and is interceding for you. This is such a comforting and secure feeling. Jesus gave us this Spirit so we would never be alone. Always remember there is no problem bigger than God.

Jesus Christ is the same yesterday and today and forever.
Hebrews 13:8 (New Living Translation)

One of my favorite hymns is Great is Thy Faithfulness. I love the words: "Great is Thy faithfulness, Oh God, my Father. There is no shadow of turning with Thee. Thou changes not. Thy compassion, it fails not. As Thou was then Thou forever shall be." Today's scripture says Jesus is the same always. Are you the same as you were even yesterday? I doubt it. We all change. The people around us change. God stays the same. He doesn't have bad days. He doesn't become bitter or even get in a better or happier mood. God stays the same as He was yesterday, today and will always be. This is not to say that He isn't disappointed when we disobey His commands. He doesn't keep changing His demands of us. They too are always the same. What a wonderful feeling, knowing God has been, will be and is always loving us and there for us. All we have to do is accept His love. It's free!

Today notice your mood. Are you acting better or worse than you did yesterday? Do you need to change anything about your personality? How would you want to act if you knew you would never change? Work on it today and try to be the person you would want to be the rest of your life. I wish I could be just like Jesus. How about you?

Keep watching and praying that you may not enter into temptation; the spirit is willing but the flesh is weak. Matthew 26:41 (New American Standard Bible)

Jesus spoke these words to his disciples, Peter, James and John, in the Garden of Gethsemane the night before His crucifixion. Jesus was very sorrowful and had asked these disciples to stand guard while He prayed. I'm certain they wanted to do this for Jesus; but when Jesus returned, they were asleep. It was then he spoke these words. When He returned the second time they were asleep again. The disciples must have been awfully tired, but surely they could have found a way to follow Jesus' desires. It is easy for me to think I would have stayed awake, but there have been so many times "my spirit was willing but my flesh was weak". His message is the same for us today. Jesus wants us to watch and pray that we follow the spirit not the flesh.

Today be aware of your actions. Notice if you do something you really feel is not your best choice. Are there times you do something without really thinking and then hope no one finds out? Can your parents or teachers trust you to do what is expected of you or do you choose to do something more enjoyable? Watch and pray about your actions. Which is stronger, your spirit or your flesh? Would Jesus be pleased with your decisions? Are you?

Love never gives up, never loses faith, is always hopeful, and endures through every circumstance. 1 Corinthians 13:7 (New Living Translation)

How appropriate it is that I am writing this on Valentine's Day 2015. As I reflect on all the love in my life, I feel so blessed. First always is the love of God, who gave us His Son, Jesus, to show us the true meaning of love. My mother was the first to show me love on earth. My father died when I was nine. I don't remember very much about him, but I am sure he loved me. I loved my sister and brother, and I think they loved me most of the time. Then God gave me your Poppa, the love of my life. Poppa and I have a special relationship and are so blessed. Like all relationships, we have had our ups and downs. However, we have "never given up, never lost faith, are always hopeful and have endured many circumstances". Because of following this scripture, our love has grown stronger every day. Poppa and I worry sometimes you see our relationship as the perfect relationship you want to find. A young man once asked his father, "Father, how will I ever find the right woman?" His father replied, "Forget finding the right woman. Focus on being the right man." (This also goes for being the right woman before finding the right man.) The only perfect relationship you will ever have is your relationship with God, and sadly it is perfect only on God's side. We too often don't work hard enough on that relationship. This relationship will guide you through all others. No mother can really explain the love she has for her children and grandchildren. You really use all of this scripture when being a parent, and the reward is so wonderful. There is also the love for our parents, siblings, our extended family and friends. The list goes on and on.

Today be aware of your feelings. Jesus told us we are to love one another and our neighbor as ourselves. If by chance you run into someone you think you do not love, remember what Abraham Lincoln said, "I don't like that man. I need to get to know him better." Look deep inside yourself and that person. Find some love. It's right there where God put it. Read 1 Corinthians 13 for the true meaning of love.

"My Father! If it is possible, let this cup of suffering be taken away from me. Yet I want your will to be done, not mine." Matthew 26:39 (New Living Translation)

Jesus spoke these words on the night before He was to be betrayed, arrested, tried and crucified. Jesus showed He was human just like us. He knew this had been God's plan from the beginning, yet He was praying it would not happen. Did He argue with God? No. He said, "Not my will, but Thy will be done." Because Jesus trusted God and His will, we have been forgiven for all of our sins. Yes, we do suffer consequences from our sins; but Jesus paid the ultimate price. This is not an easy prayer to pray. I remember when Papaw (Poppa's dad) was very sick and near death, I tried to pray this prayer but would then worry that God's will would not be mine. It was God's will for Papaw to be taken to heaven where he would no longer suffer. God's will, as always, was best. I was just being selfish and not wanting to lose Papaw. Someday it will be God's will that I join Papaw and all the others I love in heaven. Until then I will continue to strive to live according to God's will, knowing I am forgiven because His Son, Jesus Christ, did the same.

Today think about it. Is anything you are suffering today as bad as what Jesus endured for us? Is there anything in your life that you know God wants you to do but you are arguing with Him about it? Remember, God's way is the only way to go. Follow Him and I promise you will be so glad you did.

No foul language is to come from your mouth, but only what is good for building up someone in need, so that it gives grace to those who hear. Ephesians 4:29 (Holman Christian Standard Bible)

Foul language is so common now. When Poppa and I were young it was shocking when one bad word was said in a movie. What happened? Now even using the Lord's name in vain is heard too often. Foul language is never used to make someone feel better or to show your love and appreciation. It seems to be a natural thing to do when you are angry. The next time you are angry stop and think. Are you respected more by others because of your foul language? Will this situation, your life or the life of anyone else be made better by your cursing? Is a movie or television show better because they use foul language? Foul language can be a bad habit. It is offensive to those who don't use it. Others don't care. The way to not offend anyone is to just avoid using it. Use your words to build up those who hear them. Remember, a tongue has no bones but it is strong enough to break a heart. Be careful with your words.

Today pay attention to words, especially your words. Did that curse word make you win a video game? Did it help you solve a problem? Cursing seems to be contagious. Stop spreading this terrible disease. It doesn't matter how hard you try, you cannot recover a word after it has been said. Today use your words wisely. Are they pleasing to God?

***Open my eyes to see the wonderful truths in your instructions.
Psalm 119:18 (New Living Translation)***

There were so many laws in the Old Testament. Psalm 119 is the longest chapter in the Bible with 176 verses, every one of them praising the hundreds of Jewish laws delivered by Moses. The people felt if they followed all of these laws they would please God. Too often they were prouder of themselves for following these laws than they were of pleasing God. When Jesus came He said the most important law to follow was to love God with all your heart, and put no other gods before Him. He said we were to love others as much as we love ourselves. If you change the word "law" in this verse to "instructions" (as it is written in some versions of the Bible) you will find in both the Old and New Testaments God has given helpful instructions, sometimes even necessary instructions, to see wondrous things in our lives.

Today open your eyes to see some of the helpful instructions God has given us. Read the Ten Commandments (Exodus 20:1-17). I have also printed them on the next page. Those who take the time to study these commandments find they are not a list of "do nots" but are God's guide to the good life.... a life full of blessings. Jesus taught us we no longer need to follow over six hundred laws. We are mainly to love God and live according to His law because it is the right way to live. Read your bible and never stop seeking God's loving guidance.

The Ten Commandments (Exodus 20:2-17 NKJV)

1. I am the Lord your God, who brought you out of the land of Egypt, out of the house of bondage. You shall have no other gods before Me.

2. You shall not make for yourself a carved image, or any likeness of anything that is in heaven above, or that is in the earth beneath, or that is in the water under the earth; you shall not bow down to them nor serve them. For I, the Lord your God, am a jealous God, visiting the iniquity of the fathers on the children to the third and fourth generations of those who hate Me, but showing mercy to thousands, to those who love Me and keep My Commandments.

3. You shall not take the name of the Lord your God in vain, for the Lord will not hold him guiltless who takes His name in vain.

4. Remember the Sabbath day, to keep it holy. Six days you shall labor and do all your work, but the seventh day is the Sabbath of the Lord your God. In it you shall do no work: you, nor your son, nor your daughter, nor your male servant, nor your female servant, nor your cattle, nor your stranger who is within your gates. For in six days the Lord made the heavens and the earth, the sea, and all that is in them, and rested the seventh day. Therefore, the Lord blessed the Sabbath day and hallowed it.

5. Honor your father and your mother, that your days may be long upon the land which the Lord your God is giving you.

6. You shall not murder.

7. You shall not commit adultery.

8. You shall not steal.

9. You shall not bear false witness against your neighbor.

10. You shall not covet your neighbor's house; you shall not covet your neighbor's wife, nor his male servant, nor his female servant, nor his ox, nor his donkey, nor anything that is your neighbor's.

Pray in the Spirit at all times and on every occasion. Stay alert and be persistent in your prayers for all believers everywhere. Ephesians 6:18 (New Living Translation)

Jesus did not leave us alone. When we accept Him as our Lord and Savior, He sends His Holy Spirit to live within us. Jesus' Spirit knows our every thought and need even before we do. When you do something you know is wrong, you will feel an uneasiness inside of you. You might even feel a little sick to your stomach. That's because the desire to please God is built inside of you. I believe that "feeling" is the Spirit's gentle touch that keeps you on the path He has for you. We are to always be aware of this blessing, continually praying about everything. No, we don't have to stop and pray an "official" prayer to God, although that is always a wonderful thing to do. On the next few pages I am including some thoughts I have read about special prayers, especially the Lord's Prayer which was given to us by Jesus during His Sermon on the Mount. These are guides to prayer, but the best prayer is from your heart with a sincere conversation with your Lord and Savior. We can pray to God no matter what we are doing. Jesus did tell us we can go to the Father only through Him. That is why He left His Spirit with us, to pray with us and for us, in Jesus' name. How wonderful is that?

Today PRAY. Pray while you work, while you play, while you are happy, while you are sad, silently, out loud. Sometimes I even pray for help in finding a lost object. Be aware of Jesus' Holy Spirit within you. Also, don't forget to be aware of the needs of others and pray for them. God will always hear you. Now listen to Him. Who knows? You may be the answer to someone's prayer. (Don't forget to read the special prayers and thoughts about prayer written on the next six pages.)

Prayer Thoughts

"I woke up early one morning and rushed into the day. I had so much to accomplish, I didn't take time to pray. Trouble just tumbled around me and heavier came the tasks. I wondered why God didn't help me and He answered, "You didn't ask." I woke up early the next morning and I paused before entering the day. You see I had so much to accomplish, I had to take time to pray."

Any concern too small to be turned into a prayer is too small to be made into a burden. — Corrie ten Boom

Prayer isn't a last resort; it's a starting point.

Pray is not a "spare wheel" you pull out when in trouble. It is a "steering wheel" that directs the right path through life.

When you pray be sure that you also listen. You have things you want to say to God, but He also has things He wants to say to you.

"Don't just pray for God to open doors. Pray for God to close the doors in your life that need to be closed." Joyce Meyer

If you spend time praying for people instead of talking about them you will get better results.

"Do not pray for an easy life, pray for the strength to endure a difficult one" Bruce Lee

"In prayer, it is better to have a heart without words than words without a heart." John Bunyan

"Your prayer for someone may or may not change them, but it always changes YOU." Craig Groeschel

The Lord's Prayer

I cannot say "OUR" if my religion has no room for other people and their needs. I cannot say "FATHER" if I do not demonstrate this relationship in my daily life.

I cannot say "WHO ART IN HEAVEN" if all my interests and pursuits are earthly things.

I cannot say "HALLOWED BE THY NAME" if I who is called by His Name am not holy.

I cannot say "THY KINGDOM COME" if I am unwilling to give up my sovereignty and accept the will of God.

I cannot say "THY WILL BE DONE" if I am unwilling or am resentful of having Him in my life.

I cannot say "ON EARTH AS IT IS IN HEAVEN" unless I am truly ready to give myself to His service here and now.

I cannot say "GIVE US THIS DAY OUR DAILY BREAD" without expending honest efforts for it or by ignoring the needs of my fellow man.

I cannot say "FORGIVE OUR TRESPASSES AS WE FORGIVE THOSE WHO TRESPASS AGAINST US" if I continue to harbor grudges against anyone.

I cannot say "LEAD US NOT INTO TEMPTATION" if I deliberately choose to remain in a situation where I am likely to be tempted.

I cannot say "DELIVER US FROM EVIL" if I am not prepared to fight in the spiritual warfare with the weapon of prayer and with His Word.

I cannot say "THINE IS THE KINGDOM, THE POWER AND THE GLORY" if I do not give disciplined obedience, if I fear what my neighbors and friends will say or do, and if I seek my own glory first.

I cannot say "AMEN" unless I can honestly say also, "Cost what it may, this is my prayer."

Pope Francis' Five Finger Prayer

A simple guide we can use when we pray.

(1) Your thumb is nearest to you. So begin your prayers by praying for those closest to you. They are the easiest to remember. While praying for our loved ones is easy the Bible also tells us to pray for our enemies who, in a negative way, are also near us.

(2) The next finger is the pointing finger. The pointing finger reminds us of those who instruct so pray for those who teach, instruct and heal. This includes teachers, doctors, and ministers. They need support and wisdom in pointing others in the right direction. Keep them in your prayers. These men and women have great influence on society and we should pray that they display and teach godly principles in all they do.

(3) The next finger is the tallest finger. Our tallest finger reminds us of those who are in charge. Pray for the president, leaders in business and industry. These people shape our nation and guide public opinion. They need God's guidance. When the king of Nineveh prayed to God he saved his nation from destruction (Jonah 3:6-10). We should pray that our decision makers repent and seek God's will as they lead us.

(4) The fourth finger is our ring finger. The ring finger is our weakest finger, as any piano teacher will testify. It should remind us to pray for those who are weak, in trouble or in pain. They need your prayers day and night. You cannot pray too much for them.

(5) And lastly comes our little finger, the smallest finger of all. Which is where we should place ourselves in relation to God and others. By the time you have prayed for the other four groups, your own needs will be put into proper perspective and you will be able to pray for yourself more effectively.

When praying for ourselves we should first confess our sins because sin breaks fellowship with God and we don't want to be out of fellowship with Him. No matter how badly we've sin take heart and know that "If we confess our sins, He is faithful and just and will forgive us our sins and purify us from all unrighteousness." (1 John 1:9 NIV) Then we should give thanks for all the blessings we have been given.

And finally, we lay out what is on our heart, the good and the bad, and we pray that God's will be done in our life. The Father loves you very much and will always do what is best for you. Trust Him and He will lead you and cause all things to work together for the good of those who love Him. (Romans 8:28)

17th Century Nun's Prayer

(Grandmomma's Prayer)

Lord, thou knowest better than I know myself that I am growing older and will some day be old. Keep me from the fatal habit of thinking I must say something on every subject and on every occasion. Release me from craving to straighten out everybody's affairs. Make me thoughtful but not moody; helpful but not bossy. With my vast store of wisdom, it seems a pity not to use it all, but Thou knowest Lord, that I want a few friends at the end.

Keep my mind free from the recital of endless details; give me wings to get to the point. Seal my lips on my aches and pains. They are increasing and love of rehearsing them is becoming sweeter as the years go by. I dare not ask for grace enough to enjoy the tales of other's pains, but help me to endure them with patience. I dare not ask for improved memory, but for a growing humility and a lessening cocksureness when my memory seems to clash with the memories of others. Teach me the glorious lesson that occasionally I may be mistaken.

Keep me reasonably sweet; I do not want to be a saint-some of them are so hard to live with-but a sour old person is one of the crowning works of the Devil. Give me the ability to see good things in unexpected places and talents in unexpected people. And, give me, O Lord, the grace to tell them so.

Amen.

This is definitely my prayer. Please have patience with me as I strive to live this prayer. I've already lived the first sentence. I am old!

The Serenity Prayer

God grant me the serenity
To accept the things I cannot change;
Courage to change the things I can;
And wisdom to know the difference.

Living one day at a time;
Enjoying one moment at a time;
Accepting hardships as the pathway to peace;
Taking, as He did, this sinful world
As it is, not as I would have it;
Trusting that He will make all things right
If I surrender to His Will;
So that I may be reasonably happy in this life
And supremely happy with Him
Forever and ever in the next.

Amen.

This simple yet expressive prayer wasn't laid down in antiquity by one of the most famous people of his day; it was instead written in the early 1930s by Reinhold Niebuhr, an American theologian. While its wording has changed across the span of those eighty-plus years between then and now, even its earliest forms are clearly recognizable as the serenity prayer. (Snopes)

Quiet words of the wise are more to be heeded than the shouts of a ruler of fools. Ecclesiastes 9:17 (New International Version)

Your great-grandfather, George W. Ridenour, Sr. (Poppa's father), was a man of few words. He was also a very wise man with a lot of common sense. When he did speak we listened. He was not interested in praise, even though he was a much-respected man in his community. On the other hand, he had a brother who loved to talk and wanted everyone to feel he was important and better than everyone else. We loved this man, but we learned not to really pay a lot of attention to much he had to say. Which brother do you want to be?

Today notice when you speak if you are trying to impress those around you and convince them of how great you are. The truth is, the only person you should try to be better than is the person you were yesterday. Are you always shouting out advice and instructions, as I tend to do? Notice the people around you. To whom do you pay attention? I hope I won't be with you on this day. This is one on which I really need to work. I don't want people to think I am important, but I do tend to try to have all the answers to other people's problems and my advice too often falls on deaf ears. Wonder why? Maybe I should follow Harry Truman's advice: "I have found that the best advice to give your children is to find what they want and then advise them to do it." Don't count on it.

Rejoice, young man, during your childhood, and let your heart be pleasant during the days of young manhood. And follow the impulses of your heart and the desires of your eyes. Yet know that God will bring you to judgment for all these things. Ecclesiastes 11:9 (New American Standard Bible)

The first of this verse seemed like advice I wasn't sure I wanted to give you. Then came the last sentence. God will judge you. I do agree with the first sentence now. Today's young people do not seem to be able to enjoy their childhood or young years. Everyone is worried about everything. That was not God's plan. He wanted us to live life in stages. Be a kid. Be a teenager. Be a young adult. Be an adult. Then be the age of your Grandmomma and Poppa and be able to look back and have great memories of each stage. You will find your best memories will be the ones you know are pleasing to God.

Today ask yourself, "Am I making the best of this day of my life?" Do not waste it. Take a break from the television or video game. Do at least one thing to go into your memory bank as something to tell your children and grandchildren, or nieces and nephews if you do not have children. Remember, you will only live this day once. Begin every day with a determination to be a blessing to as many people as possible. Then you cannot go wrong.

So we do not lose heart. Though our outer part is wasting away, our inner self is being renewed day by day. 2 Corinthians 4:16 (English Standard Version)

When you are Poppa and Grandmomma's age this verse really hits home, especially after spending three days at Disney. Our outer part seems to be worn out, but our inner selves are feeling so blessed. It is true that most of my Disney trips lately have been enjoyed from a wheelchair. However, I honestly believe my inner self is more appreciative of everything there, especially my family with me. Disney is majestic, but it will be nothing compared to the place God has prepared for us. At Disney, the buildings and rides often need repaired. The toys and souvenirs sometimes break. Nothing is permanent, not even the smiles on everyone's face. Not so in heaven. Everything there will be forever, and we will meet our Savior face to face (without a wheelchair!)

Today look for a possession you have that will not break or cannot be lost? How about your inner being? Are you growing more mature and more aware of consequences of your actions and feelings? Be aware of your feelings and decide which ones are preparing you to be ready to meet Jesus and be in paradise forever. Jesus told us that we can only get to Heaven through Him. If we have faith in Jesus we will not only make it to heaven, but we will learn to live through all the trials we face on earth and be grateful for each day we are given. Someday Poppa and I look forward to seeing you in Heaven, but not anytime soon. Our outer parts are still working. God isn't through with us yet.

Take my yoke upon you, and learn from me, for I am gentle and lowly in heart, and you will find rest for your souls. For my yoke is easy and my burden is light. Matthew 11:29-30 (English Standard Version)

When a yoke (heavy bar of wood) was connected to two animals used for plowing in biblical times, it was easier for the animals to get more work done. Jesus tells us if we connect our yoke to Him, He will make our burdens light and easy. So, what have I been doing about this verse? I have been worrying about it and looking up all references to it, wanting to be certain you know how this verse can influence your life. I'm afraid I had started trying to make an impressive book for you rather than just opening my heart to you. Thus, the worry and concern. I must learn if I follow the words of our Savior, the heavy yoke of worry is gone. That is an ongoing challenge for me. Notice Jesus didn't say He would take away our yokes (burdens). He said He would replace our heavy yoke for one easy and light. Jesus was telling the people it was not necessary to carry the heavy burden of following the many trivial laws of the Sanhedrin and priests. You cannot earn your way to heaven. You only need to accept Jesus as the Son of God and your Savior. Then you will desire to follow His commandments. "And his commandments are not burdensome." (1 John 5:3 NIV)

Today notice if something in your life is a heavy burden on your heart. Are you worried about your school work or a problem with your parents, friends or siblings? Maybe you feel your life is lacking something. Remember this verse. If you turn to Jesus and His teachings, He can make this burden lighter. He helped me realize I was making this verse too hard. Maybe you will also see your problem is not really as bad as you think. Trust Him, ask Him, then listen and He will lighten your load.

(Read Ad-lib on Next Page)

(Read Previous Page)

Ad-lib to Matthew 11:28-30

This is a perfect example of what I am trying to teach you. Learn your Bible verses and you will be reminded of them at the right time. This morning (a few weeks after writing about this verse) I was up early with lots of worries on my mind. While I was praying I had these thoughts and wrote them down to add to this verse:

His yoke is easy!!! While praying this morning I noticed how uptight I was. I relaxed my shoulders and could feel the load on my shoulders disappear. I need to work on this. Every time I feel my shoulders and neck tightening because of stress, I will try to remember these verses (Matthew 11:28-30). Jesus' yoke keeps me connected to my Heavenly Father who will carry my load for me, if I will accept His help and not try to handle everything myself. It has taken me many years and many heartaches to finally realize I have never had any problem that God has not helped me handle. With every trial God has made me stronger and love Him more. He will do the same for you if you will let Him.

Urge bondslaves to be subject to their own masters in everything, to be well-pleasing, not argumentative, not pilfering, but showing all good faith so that they will adorn the doctrine of God our Savior in every respect. Titus 2:9-10 (New American Standard Bible)

In Paul's letter to Titus he shares many suggestions on spreading the teachings of Jesus and influencing others to do the same. As slavery was common in the time of the early church and about half of those who lived in the Roman Empire were slaves, good works from a Christian slave would be attractive to a non-Christian master. Sometimes actions speak louder than words. I realize now how my life was influenced by the actions of good Christian people, even if I didn't realize it at the time. Thank God slavery is no longer accepted. However, we are all to be servants of God. I pray I will be a servant of which God is proud.

Today notice your actions. Are you acting as someone who will be a good influence on those around you? How would you feel if you were someone else watching your words and actions? Will people know you are a Christian by how you live? Let your life preach more loudly than your lips. "The world is changed by your example, not your opinion." Pablo Coelho

Very truly I tell you, unless a kernel of wheat falls to the ground and dies, it remains only a single seed. But if it dies, it produces many seeds. John 12:24 (New International Version)

Jesus spoke these words soon before his arrest and crucifixion. He was predicting his death. When a seed dies it produces fruit. Jesus was speaking of Himself as the seed of wheat. His death would produce much fruit and result in many living for God. Jesus had to suffer a terrible death so He could be resurrected and go to prepare a wonderful eternal place for us. His seed lives on forever. What seeds are you planting?

Today notice if you are spreading the seeds of love, kindness, faith, compassion, and the list goes on and on. Or are you spreading seeds of anger, discontentment, sloppiness, and that list can be even longer and easier to spread. Strive to always plant a beautiful garden which will bless everyone around you and will make Jesus proud.

"Why do you look at the speck of sawdust in your brother's eye and pay no attention to the plank in your own eye? How can you say to your brother, 'Let me take the speck out of your eye,' when all the time there is a plank in your own eye? Matthew 7:3-4 (New International Version)

Good question. I doubt many, if any, days pass without this verse being ignored. I don't think we do it on purpose. We truly are not aware of some of our short-comings. How many times have I corrected one of you, only to realize I have probably done the same thing? It is so much easier to see faults in others.

Today every time you criticize someone or judge someone for their actions or looks, look at yourself. Do you have anything that could be criticized as well? As my Mother always said, "There is so much good in the worst of us and so much bad in the best of us; that it hardly behooves any of us to talk about the rest of us.

.... "eXcept ye be converted, and become as little children, ye shall not enter into the kingdom of heaven. Matthew 18:3 (King James Bible)

When I read this verse separate from the rest in the chapter, I felt Jesus was telling us again we should have the innocence and beliefs of a child. However, in reading the complete chapter I found Jesus was answering His disciples when they asked who would be the greatest in the kingdom of Heaven. Jesus answered, "Therefore, whoever takes the lowly position of this child is the greatest in the kingdom of heaven." Jesus wanted them to lay aside their ambitions and pride and be willing to take the "lowly position" of a child. Poppa and I saw the best movie, "God is Not Dead". In the movie, a young pre-law student was in a psychology class, and the professor asked everyone in the class to sign a paper saying God is dead. Even though he knew he would fail this class and would possibly ruin his chance to get into law school, he refused to sign. The professor told him he would still have a chance to pass the class if he could prove God was alive. He chose to take the challenge. His family was very much against this, and his girlfriend even broke up with him because he was "throwing away" his chance for the career he had planned. The students in the class thought he was maybe overreacting. He believed strongly in God and took a very "lowly position" because of his child-like faith. He presented his beliefs to the class, and he was not sorry. I'll not give you the ending. You must find this movie and watch it. It was in the theaters but is now on television.

Today start your search for this movie. It really is a good movie. In the meantime, think about your faith. Would you sign a form saying God is dead to get something you want? Are you a Christian because it makes you special? Or are you a Christian because you believe in God and know His way is the best way to live? We are all loved by our Heavenly Father, none more or none less. We are all His children. Let us all strive to live in a way to make our Heavenly Father proud.

Yet you do not know what your life will be like tomorrow. You are just a vapor that appears for a little while and then vanishes away. James 4:14 (New American Standard Bible)

The thought that I am just a vapor waiting to disappear at first sounds a little creepy. However, in God's time that is right. How long is forever? We are on this earth such a short time compared to forever. Thinking of it in those terms makes me want to take advantage of every moment. We do not know what tomorrow will bring to our earthly bodies. Poppa and I have proven that in our near-death health problems. Those times have made me even more aware of the importance of living every day in a way pleasing to my Heavenly Father so I will be able to spend eternity with Him (and with you).

Today be aware of your actions. Is there anything you would be sorry you did or did not do if you did not have tomorrow? You have many more tomorrows to enjoy. Don't waste any of them with regrets. We never know what will happen and we should live each day as if it is our last. Is there anyone with whom you need to make peace? This may sound a little morbid. The truth is, living every day as if it is your last only makes you appreciate the day and enjoy it more. Make every day pleasing to God and enjoy the life He has given you. "Love like there is no tomorrow; and if tomorrow comes, love again" ….... Quote by Max Lucado

..............."Zaccheus, come down immediately. I must stay at your house today." Luke 19:5 (New International Version)

As I'm sure you have determined, I did choose this verse because it started with a Z. I'm glad I did. I love the message. Zacchaeus was a Jew working for the Roman Government, collecting taxes from the Jews. He would charge more than required by law and keep it for himself, which was definitely a sin. He was extremely despised by his fellow Jews. Zacchaeus was a short man and had climbed a tree so he could see Jesus; thus, the common saying "going out a limb for someone". Imagine Zacchaeus' surprise when Jesus called him by name, telling him to climb down because Jesus was going to stay at his house. Jesus did not choose a leader of the church or a respected member of the community. He chose a despised sinner. Through this example we are shown Jesus came to save sinners, and we all do sin. This is really a hard one for me. As an adult, I can easily be comfortable in befriending a sinner and showing and sharing God's love. We may hate the sin, but we love the sinner. It is harder to tell my young grandchildren to be friends with someone who could be a bad influence on them. Just as I was typing this, I realized I have special grandchildren who could be a good influence for others. Set good examples for others, but avoid the bad influence some could have on you.

Today think about it. Do you know someone going astray who could be encouraged just by a smile or kind word? Always be aware of your opportunity to set a good example for others and show them God is love and His way is the way to go.

Chapter Five

Above all else guard your heart because everything you do flows from it. Proverbs 4:23 (New International Version)

The heart. Isn't that an organ in your body? If our heart stops, every other part of our body stops. Now that is a powerful and important organ. We also use the "heart" to symbolize our inner spirit which also keeps us going. I have heard it said that a happy heart is a healthy heart. When we have a happy attitude we not only feel better ourselves, but we make those around us happy as well. An old Cherokee proverb tells about a battle of two wolves going on inside of us. One wolf is evil. It is anger, jealousy, greed, resentment, lies, inferiority and ego. The other wolf is good. It is joy, peace, love, hope, humility, kindness, empathy and truth. Which wolf wins?........The one you feed.

Today feed the good wolf inside you. How hard could that be? Believe me, some days it is really hard. It is so much easier to feed that evil wolf, but the end result adds only sadness to your life. Try this. Just smile. Sometimes it's all that's needed in a high stress, going to blow your top moment. It feels so good, even if it is a fake smile. Smiles are contagious. It also will help get rid of the evil thoughts that come your way. Then everything that flows from your heart will be pleasing to God, yourself and everyone around you. No matter how you feel, get up, dress up, show up and never give up. Share your happy heart!

(Read note on next page)

Note about Previous Page

God speaks to us always. We just need to listen. As I am proofreading this book, Poppa and I are on a five-week cruise. Poppa absolutely loves cruising and loves working on the book he is writing for you while on the ship. He is giving you his summary and opinions of the Bible. He has been working on it every day for at least eight years, and it is very interesting. I am in our cabin feeling really bad.... or at least I thought I was. I had made up my mind to just stay in here all day and I guess be pitiful. I decided I had enough energy to at least proofread a few pages of this book. I felt the previous page needed a little something else, and I went to the section where I have thoughts and sayings I like. Of all things, I had to see the one that said, "No matter how you feel, get up, dress up, show up and never give up." I definitely did not want to see that today. I am so tired. But, do you know what? "It's right. I will only live this day once. I will put on my happy heart and let everything good flow from it.

LATER: We are now in our last week of the cruise. We have had one of the best trips of our lives and have truly enjoyed our time together. I am so glad I read the statement that got me out of bed and made me realize I have a lot of living still to do. We had such a wonderful day in Curacao yesterday and are feeling so blessed that God gave us the strength and opportunity to add this as another wonderful memory. A picture on the author's page shows how happy I was in Curacao and answers my challenge in your "letter to my grandchildren". Your Poppa loves life better than anyone I have ever known. I hope each of you will be like him. No matter how you feel, get up, dress up, show up and never give up. I promise you will be glad you did. I was!

Be always joyful. Be unceasing in prayer. In every circumstance of life be thankful; for this is God's will in Christ Jesus. I Thessalonians 5:16-18 (Weymouth New Testament)

Have you ever known someone who seems to be happy all the time? I have. Her name was Yvonne Wilson. She was a member of our church and was in the last stages of cancer when I first got to know her. She always had a pleasant smile, even though she was so frail. Mrs. Wilson was a widow with no children, and I told her to please call me if she ever felt down and just needed to talk. She thanked me for the offer, but said she didn't have bad times. She was grateful for her life and all her friends and was at peace. This was not a lady with no problems. She was dying of cancer. She was a person who, even though she has been dead for several years now, is still an inspiration to me. I have a long way to go to find her peace, but I do think of her often when I get discouraged.

Today notice your attitude. Are you optimistic, or do you tend to be a pessimist? Who is the most optimistic person you know? It really is not easy to think of one. Poppa and I did think of a high school friend who has been joyful always any time we have been around him. This man, Eddie Rains, is truly a man of God. When Poppa was so sick from Whipple surgery and blood clots, Eddie would always check on him, even though he himself was being treated for cancer at that time. Eddie always gave us a feeling of peace, knowing he was praying for us. Sadly, it is easier to think of people who are pessimistic. Which do you want to be? When you follow the verse for today, pray without ceasing and give thanks in all situations, you will find it is easier to be joyful always. Maybe someday you can be someone's inspiration like Yvonne Wilson and Eddie Rains are to me.

Consider it pure joy, my brothers and sisters, whenever you face trials of many kinds, because you know the testing of your faith produces perseverance. Let perseverance finish its work so that you will be mature and complete, not lacking anything. James 1:2-4 (New International Version)

When something goes wrong in your life is your first emotion pure joy? Of course not. However, it was after a very rough time in my life, when I had no other choice but to turn to God, that I became a true believer. I was given the faith which has brought me through so many "trials of many kinds". I do not believe God causes bad things to happen so we will turn to Him. However, I do believe He uses those times to draw us closer to Him and see His love and His help in all situations. Too often, when everything is going well, we tend to forget to even pray. Hard times have not only taught me to persevere but also to pray what may seem to be impossible prayers. I have learned no prayer is too difficult for God, and I feel He wants us to feel free to be persistent in our prayers. Some of my constant prayers have not yet been answered, but I keep praying and know that God will answer these prayers in His own time if it is His will. Jesus said if we have faith the size of a mustard seed, which is the smallest of seeds and becomes a large tree, nothing will be impossible for us (Matthew 17:20). Our faith should also be as persistent as the mustard seed. It is very fast growing and doesn't stop growing until it takes over all land around it. God wants our faith to take over our lives and spread to the lives of all around us.

Today think about problems you have had. Did you or someone else learn from them? Did anything good happen because of the problem? You may not see it now, but I promise you will when you are my age. With God's help, you did survive. Don't dwell on these problems. Learn from them. Believe it or not, I now thank God for the problems I have had, for being there for me and causing my faith in Him to become even stronger.

Do you not know that you are God's temple and that God's Spirit dwells in you? 1 Corinthians 3:16 (English Standard Version)

This verse had a different meaning to me when I read it without reading the entire chapter. I understood it to simply mean that my body was God's temple. This was not what Paul had in mind when he wrote this letter to the local church in Corinth, scolding them because they, the body of Christ, were bickering amongst themselves and being less than a good example of Christians. Paul spoke to me in this same letter thousands of years later, making me aware that I too am God's temple. God's Spirit lives within me and wants me to live for Him. If I abuse my body I will destroy it by ruining my health, and then what good am I for God?

Today be aware of your body, inside and out. Are you feeding it in a way to keep it healthy, both spiritually and physically? Are you setting a good example of a Christian? Are you keeping your body healthy by eating right, exercising enough and keeping it free from harmful substances? Is your body a temple in which you would want to house God's Spirit? God's Spirit is with us no matter what, as long as we accept Jesus as God's Son and our Savior. That is why I want to strive to make my body a temple in which God's Spirit will be proud to reside. I have a long way to go, but I know now that a healthy body will help me live a better life for Christ. How about you?

***Each of you should give what you have decided in your heart to give, not reluctantly or under compulsion, for God loves a cheerful giver.
2 Corinthians 9:7 (New International Version)***

I love to give. That is, I love to give presents to family and friends, tips to everyone and donations to organizations. Of course, I want to give my share to our church. That type of giving is easy, especially if you are blessed to have the resources. Giving my time isn't that easy. I am so selfish with my time, and I hate taking time away from Poppa and our regular activities to obligate myself to anything. Reading this verse again helped my guilt somewhat. We all have different gifts. We each should decide in our heart the best way we can give. Some people love working in organizations and doing good deeds away from home. I can cheerfully give my time to others by writing cards to friends who are sick or just need to know someone cares. I also should always be aware of those around me who need my time. Sometimes the person who has been there for everyone else needs someone to be there for them.

Today consider how you give your time or resources to help others. Are you pleased with your answer? Decide in your heart how you can give and then give cheerfully. It doesn't have to be a big chore or a lot of money. Just try to be cheerful and maybe giving will become a joyful and natural activity in your life. I promise it will make you feel even better than the one to which you give.

For God so loved the world, that he gave his only begotten Son, that whosoever believeth in him should not perish, but have everlasting life. John 3:16 (King James Bible)

This is probably one of the most familiar of all Bible verses. It truly says it all. Read it over again. God made us. He loved us, but we kept messing up all through the Old Testament (and sadly still do). Then He sent His Only Son to show us the way. He let His Son die a terrible death on the cross so all of our sins will be forgiven. This Son, Jesus Christ, through His resurrection, revealed to us that we will have everlasting life with Him and His Father in Heaven. All we have to do is believe in Him. What a powerful verse!

Today say this verse over and over again. Listen to the words. Do not let Jesus' death be in vain. Love Him as much as He and His Father love you.

….. God is our refuge and strength, an ever-present help in times of trouble. Psalm 46:1 (New International Version)

Ever-present? Yes, God is ever-present in our lives. The sad truth is we are not ever-aware of this fact. Too many times I have fretted over problems in my life without even thinking about God. It is when I remember this verse that I feel His presence, His protection and His strength.

Today be as ever-aware of God's presence as He is ever-present. Be aware that God is in the room with you. If you have a problem with your school work, ask Him to help you concentrate and find the answer. If you are having a disagreement with a friend or sibling, ask God to help you work through it. In anything that happens to you today, be aware that God is by your side. As encouraging as that is, it can also be a little unnerving. Sometimes I wish He could just close His eyes to my actions and His ears to my thoughts. As much as He helps us, He also forgives us. Now that is a wonderful feeling.

Happy moments, PRAISE GOD
Difficult moments, SEEK GOD
Quiet moments, WORSHIP GOD
Painful moments, TRUST GOD
Every moment, THANK GOD
Rick Warren

Humble yourselves, therefore, under God's mighty hand, that He may lift you up in due time. Cast all your anxiety on Him because He cares for you. 1 Peter 5:6-7 (New International Version)

Just before Peter wrote this verse he wrote "God opposes the proud but shows favor to the humble." Maybe that is because God wants us to trust Him and not be so proud and think we can live our lives and handle our problems without Him. He shows favor to the humble because they cast their anxieties on Him. I know how frustrated I get when I try to help one of you and you appear to ignore me. Imagine how God, with all His love for us and His mighty power to help, feels when we appear to ignore him and are too proud to ask for His guidance and try to handle everything by ourselves.

Today (and always) cast your anxieties on God and know He cares for you. Think of something that has been bothering you. Take it to the Lord in prayer. The verse says He will lift you up in due time. This means you may not get your answer today, or even tomorrow; but you will be able to handle it because you know it is in God's hands. I'll have to admit this is where I have a problem. I have trouble not trying to take the problem back or giving God advice about how to handle it. I sure do need to work on being humble.

It is by grace you have been saved through faith, and this not from yourself. It is a gift from God--- not by works so that no one can boast. Ephesians 2:8-9 (New International Version)

This gift seems too good to be true. God saves us from sin and gives us eternal life just because we have faith in Him and His Son. We don't receive this gift because of all our good works. God doesn't want us doing good works trying to get to heaven or impress others. All He asks is that we believe in Him and His Son. All we have to do is accept this wonderful gift. When we accept this gift, good works come naturally.

Just for today notice when you do a good deed if you are wanting praise for it. That is the natural reaction, but not the one pleasing to God. Do something today that needs to be done, and then work on feeling good because you did something pleasing to God without boasting to others. It is a hard assignment. You may make it through today without telling you did it, but tomorrow will be harder. If you need to feel proud, be proud that you were able to do something helpful without being praised.

Judge not, and you shall not be judged; condemn not, and you shall not be condemned; forgive, and you shall be forgiven. Luke 6:37 (English Standard Version)

Do you usually have an opinion of someone you meet? Even if you don't really notice their appearance, which is unlikely, you will notice if they are pleasant or not. Do you judge them by their appearance before you even know their personality? Do you condemn them if they have different opinions and a life style different than yours? A true genius, Albert Einstein, once said, "Everyone is a genius. But if you judge a fish by its ability to climb a tree, it will live its whole life believing that it is stupid." How true. What about forgiveness? That's a hard one. Jesus died on the cross so we would be forgiven. For us to forgive people who have hurt us is not easy, but is necessary. It is what God asks of us and what He does for us. This may be difficult to do, but we all need to work on it. In the blink of the eye everything can change. You never know when you won't have that chance again. Don't wait to forgive and to love.

Today be aware of your opinions of those around you. Do you judge them at all? How would you feel about yourself if you were the judge of your actions and appearance? It is so easy to see what we consider faults in others but not in ourselves. Is there someone you need to forgive? Pray for that person. Maybe your heart will soften and you will find the peace promised if we trust in God and His ways. Don't waste another day judging others. Your life will be so much better if you strive to accept everyone as God accepts you.

Keep your lives free from the love of money and be content with what you have, because God has said, "Never will I leave you, never will I forsake you." Hebrews 13:5 (New International Version)

Some people love to spend money on all types of luxuries and pleasures, while others love to save every penny they earn. I have heard of people who have lived their whole lives as paupers, and after their deaths are found to be millionaires. It is always wise to save some of your money, and it is also okay to spend it. Your love for money is only a problem when money is more important to you than your love for God. It is so sad to see people who are never content and never feel they have enough. This is not a new problem. Adam and Eve lived in Paradise and still were not content. They just had to eat that forbidden fruit. We know what a problem that caused for all of us.

Today be aware of what gives you peace. Are you content when you get a new "thing", or do you soon tire of it and think of something else you want or think you need? Do you feel lots of money will make you happy? I have known too many people who have more money than most and still never seem to be happy. Think of the blessings you have that didn't cost a penny. If you had to trade a blessing, would you choose something bought or something God has provided, such as your parents or siblings? Would you trade your good health for a new car? God wants us to enjoy life and have nice things. However, God knows things will not provide the life He wants for us. I have learned that nothing in my life has ever given me joy, peace and contentment without the love of God and the desire to live according to His will. I know He will never leave me or forsake me, supplying all my needs, not wants. I pray you will accept His peace also, always putting God first in your lives.

Let the words of my mouth and the meditation of my heart be acceptable in thy sight, Oh Lord, my strength and my redeemer. Psalm 19:14 (King James Bible)

Wouldn't it be a wonderful world if everything we said and all of our thoughts were acceptable to God? It is easier to watch what we say than it is what we think. The verse goes on to say that God is "my strength and my redeemer". He will give us strength to change our attitudes, thus changing our thoughts, words and actions. Again, this can only be done if we let Him. I wish God literally made me do the right thing. That isn't the way He works. He leads but has given us a free will.

Today be aware of every word that comes from your mouth. Is it pleasing to God? How about your thoughts? Do you need to work on your attitude and acceptance of others? Notice how thoughts and words pleasing to your Heavenly Father make life much more pleasant for you and everyone around you.

Make a joyful noise unto the LORD, all ye lands.
Serve the LORD with gladness: come before his presence with singing. Know ye that the LORD he is God: it is he that hath made us, and not we ourselves; we are his people, and the sheep of his pasture. Enter into his gates with thanksgiving, and into his courts with praise: be thankful unto him, and bless his name. For the LORD is good; his mercy is everlasting; and his truth endureth to all generations. Psalm 100:1-5 (King James Bible)

No, this is not one verse. It is Chapter 100 in the book of Psalms. When I was a very young girl it was our assignment in Sunday School to memorize the 100th Psalm. I did and have remembered it all of my long life. As it says, "His love endures forever and His faithfulness continues through all generations." He loved my Granny, my mother and me. Now God is there for all my children and grandchildren. He loved my father and grandfathers and another grandmother also, but they went to live with Him before I could know them. It is such a wonderful feeling to know God's love continues forever. This chapter and all of the words of the Bible were inspired by God and will be there for all generations until Jesus returns. You can't always have the Bible with you. You will find there is so much comfort in being able to recall a verse.

Today think of any verses you have memorized. If there are none, find one. Memorize it today and remember it always. Someday you may share it with your grandchildren. In fact, why not learn the 100th Psalm and make a joyful noise unto the Lord, serve Him, praise Him, give thanks to Him and embrace His love and faithfulness which endures through all generations.

"Now my soul is troubled, and what shall I say? 'Father, save me from this hour'? No, it was for this very reason I came to this hour. John 12:27 (New International Version)

After reading the complete Chapter 12 and also commentaries about this verse, my emotions are all over the place. I have read all of this before but evidently have not really given it as much thought as I do when wondering what part to share with you in this little space. Jesus was a human being. He had feelings just like you and me. He also came to show us that human beings do not have to give into their sometimes-self-centered emotions. Jesus was not the mighty warrior the Jews had expected as their Messiah. In fact, He did not want the worship and praise the crowd who did believe He was the Messiah wanted to give Him. He had come to glorify God and to lead the people to know God and to live according to His commands. Jesus came to die for all of our sins and to tell us about the eternal life we are promised if we believe in Him and live by His examples. No, Jesus was not anxious to die the horrible death on the cross. He may have even been afraid. Jesus showed us how much He loved us and trusted God when He said, "Not my will, but Thine be done." Yes, "God showed how much he loved us by sending his one and only Son into the world so that we might have eternal life through Him." 1 John 4:9 (New Living Translation)

Today take time to stop and think about how much our Savior, Jesus Christ, suffered to save us from our sins and to give us the promise of eternal life. No matter how bad you may feel, your pain cannot compare to the pain Jesus suffered on the cross, not to even mention the beating He suffered and the pain of carrying the cross before even being placed upon the cross. Most importantly, remember He did all of this for us willingly. It is because Jesus lived and died for us that we are able to live a life with assurance of God's guidance, His comfort and help in our times of need and the promise of an everlasting life.

Or do you think lightly of the riches of His kindness and tolerance and patience, not knowing that the kindness of God leads you to repentance? Romans 2:4 (New American Standard Bible)

In this letter Paul was asking the people of the church in Rome why they were so judgmental of others when they acted the same way themselves. He reminded them that God was the only one who should judge; and God's kindness, tolerance and patience of them should not be taken lightly, but should be an example of how they should act. It is so easy to judge others, not even being aware that we have also acted in the same way. Even though God is aware of our sins, He wishes to guide us to do better, not to judge and condemn us. God's grace should lead us to repent of our sins, not to judge and condemn others.

Today when you start to judge someone, ask yourself if you have acted in the same way or in a similar way. Do you think God has seen this and still loves you and wants you to act differently in the future? Try to use the same tolerance, patience and kindness to others. Be an example not a judge. "A good man apologizes for his mistakes of the past. A great man corrects them."- Johann Wolfgang von Goethe

Peace I leave with you; my peace I give you. I do not give to you as the world gives. Do not let your hearts be troubled and do not be afraid. John 14:27 (New International Version)

We are told in the Bible over and over again that we are not to be afraid. Jesus gave us the above verse just before His crucifixions. He died on the cross so we would be forgiven of our sins and could live in peace with our fellow men. It is such a shame that very few find this peace while they are young. I know I certainly wish I had. I have spent so much time being afraid of what might happen to my family and to me. It sadly has just been in the recent years I have truly found peace in my faith in Jesus Christ. Now I honestly can quickly talk myself out of fear once I remember God is in control and has solved so many problems for me. He may not have done it exactly the way I would have chosen, but He has given me peace that can only come from trusting and obeying the Savior of all. The world will always give you troubles, but God sent His Son to give us peace. It starts out hard to accept; but soon, if you will make a conscious effort to remember the times you have made it through other problems, the feeling of peace will come easier.

Today know there is nothing to fear but fear itself (Franklin D. Roosevelt). Instead of noticing how big your problem is, remember how big your God is. Start while you are young knowing Jesus meant it when He said, "Do not be afraid. I leave you with my peace." This is not to say life will always be peaceful. That would be wonderful but very unlikely. There will always be stressful times when it may be hard for you to find the peace Jesus offers. This is when you truly need to seek the love and strength from Jesus and know everything will be okay in His time and for His purpose.

Quenched the power of fire, escaped the edge of the sword, were made strong out of weakness, became mighty in war, put foreign armies to flight. Hebrews 11:34 (English Standard Version)

It is amazing how many believers were in the Old Testament, and how strong their faith, even though they did not have the written Gospel we have today. They were not able to read about the many acts of faith that literally enabled everything written in the verse above. The author of Hebrews 11 (which no one knows) gave many examples of men of faith and closed this chapter by stating that he didn't have time to tell about Gideon, Barak, Samson and Jephthah, about David and Samuel and the prophets, who through faith conquered kingdoms, administered justice, and gained what was promised. Not only did they do this and what is written in the verse for today, some faced ridicule and were put in prisons. They were even put to death by stoning, sawed in two, killed by the sword and other hideous deaths. They wandered in the deserts and mountains, living in caves and in holes in the ground. The complete stories are written throughout the Bible. It is sad to me that now, even though the Bible is available to everyone and these examples of faith are made clear, the number of believers is so small and their faith so weak. We are truly blessed that even when we lack faith, God is faithful. God tells us to be courageous as we face the dangers and the battles of life. We may not always travel in safe territory but we will never be alone. Our God is with us wherever we go.

Today examine your faith. What is faith? "Now faith is confidence in what we hope for and assurance about what we do not see." Hebrews 11:1 (New International Version). When in doubt, ask for God's guidance. He has promised to be with you and lead you in the way you should go. Please read the beautiful Twenty-Third Psalm on the next page. This is a psalm many of us have memorized, and is such comfort in times of need.

The Twenty-Third Psalm

{A Psalm of David.}
King James Bible

The LORD is my shepherd; I shall not want.

He maketh me to lie down in green pastures: he leadeth me beside the still waters.

He restoreth my soul: he leadeth me in the paths of righteousness for his name's sake.

Yea, though I walk through the valley of the shadow of death, I will fear no evil: for thou art with me; thy rod and thy staff they comfort me.

Thou preparest a table before me in the presence of mine enemies: thou anointest my head with oil; my cup runlet over.

Surely goodness and mercy shall follow me all the days of my life: and I will dwell in the house of the LORD forever.

Rejoice in our confident hope. Be patient in trouble, and keep on praying. Romans 12:12 (New Living Translation)

I really hate to admit this, but there have been times when I felt like just giving up. I would get so discouraged when my health seemed to be so bad and I knew it would never get better. Truthfully, this has happened more than once; but I have seen, with prayer and patience, God has renewed by hope. I am learning that my only disability in life is a bad attitude. When we believe in Christ we are assured of His love and know He is with us through all our trials. You cannot make yourselves glad when times are bad, but you can rule the direction of your thoughts. Poppa is really good at keeping a good attitude when I know he is not happy, not to say he doesn't have some bad days. We all are human and have feelings, but we also all have the hope of a better day. Keep praying, be patient and rejoice in your confident hope.

Today test your mind. Think of something you have been wanting to happen. Now be negative. Decide in your heart that it will never happen. How does it feel? Now be positive that someday it will happen, even if it takes longer than you hoped or even if something different and better happens. Just the confident hope is cause for rejoicing. Having a positive mental attitude is asking how something can be done rather than saying it can't be done. Eleanor Roosevelt once said, "You can often change your circumstances by changing your attitude." Life is so much happier when we don't give up. It's true, we may not get exactly what we had in mind; but we will be able to handle all things through Christ who gives us strength.

So do not worry, saying, 'What shall we eat?' or 'What shall we drink?' or 'What shall we wear?' For the pagans run after all these things, and your heavenly Father knows that you need them. But seek first his kingdom and his righteousness, and all these things will be given to you as well. Therefore, do not worry about tomorrow, for tomorrow will worry about itself. Each day has enough trouble of its own. Matthew 6:31-34 (New International Version)

Poppa's father gave this advice in every situation. I could never know what he was really thinking, but his outward appearance always had a calming effect on all of us. When I look back on my life, even on just yesterday, I see so much time I wasted worrying about something that did not happen. Statistics show that a great majority of things feared will never take place. Worrying does not make one thing happen or not happen. It only keeps you from enjoying time you will never have again. Instead of worrying about where life will take you, remember God is already there. He is in control.

Today be aware of every time you worry about anything. Is there something you can do right now that will help the situation? If so, do it. If not, write your worry on a piece of paper and save it. In a few weeks check the paper and see if it really happened. Was it really worth the worry? Have faith and remember Papaw's advice. "Take care of today and tomorrow will take care of itself."

The more the words, the less the meaning, and how does that profit anyone? Ecclesiastes 6:11 (New International Version)

Poppa always said that the first five minutes of a closing argument or any speech are very important. People tend to stop listening after just a few minutes. Have you been around people who just keep talking and you find your mind wondering off to other things? I know you have. You have been around me. I wish I would remember this verse when I start on my advice talks or even just talking about my experiences.

Today listen to not only what others say but also to what you say. Are you wasting words? How many times do you use "I, me or my"? Remember, when you talk, you are only repeating things you already know. When you listen, you may learn something new. Believe me, this is easier said than done, at least for me.

Grandmomma's Ad-lib: Okay, I have already admitted that I have trouble following this verse. I was proud this was one of the shortest "lessons" in the book. However, as I was proof reading I realized just how many times "I" and "my" were there. Looks like I (there it is again) really do need to work on this. You have to give me a break. This is a book about "my" feelings and "I" sure do have a lot of them. At least you can put the book down when you have had enough.

.......Unto thee, O God, do we give thanks, unto thee do we give thanks: for that thy name is near thy wondrous works declare. Psalm 75:1 (King James Bible)

God's wondrous works are literally everywhere. No place in the entire world is without God's wonders. Even if we are in a dark room all alone, we are a part of God's wondrous works. Poppa and I have been blessed to travel to many different places. It is impossible to be anywhere without giving thanks and praise to God and feeling His presence. Every morning we see the beauty of Florida from our bedroom window, the ocean, the birds, the sky which is different every morning. In fact, this morning I just saw a dolphin swim by. Then at nighttime we see the beautiful sunset, and we thank God for another day. We still miss the beautiful hills of Tennessee, the seasons, the spring flowers, the autumn leaves, and the list goes on and on. Thank you, God.

Today open your eyes to the wonders of God. Say "thank you" each time. Yes, nature is beautiful. Also, be aware of the wonders of your family and friends. God has made everything beautiful in its time. (Ecclesiastes 3:11 NIV)

Very early in the morning, while it was still dark, Jesus got up, left the house and went off to a solitary place to pray. Mark 1:35 (New International Version)

I love waking up early in the morning while it is still dark outside. It is so peaceful. This is a wonderful time to talk to God. It is even more meaningful since I read this scripture, knowing that over 2000 years ago Jesus did the same. Sometimes I even feel we are praying together. Jesus was human. He prayed to God just as He taught us to do. He needed guidance from God, and He also had so much for which to give God praise.

Today start your day with a prayer. It is also always good to start the day remembering "This is the day that the LORD has made; let us rejoice and be glad in it. Psalm 118:24 (English Standard Version). One small positive thought in the morning can change your entire day. Make prayer your key in the morning and your lock at night. Then enjoy your day, knowing Jesus will be with you all the way.

Wait patiently for the LORD. Be brave and courageous. Yes, wait patiently for the LORD. Psalm 27:14 (New Living Translation)

I read about a person who worked in a clothing factory. The thread in her machine became tangled and she tried to fix it herself, only to make it worse. Her supervisor saw the problem and told her she should have asked for help before she got it into such a mess. Too often we don't think God is working fast enough and we try to fix the problem alone. Abraham's wife, Sarah, did this. She was concerned she would not be able to give Abraham the child God had promised, and she asked Abraham to have a child by her maidservant. This child's (Ismael) ancestors (Muslims) are still a cause of friction with Sarah's son's (Isaac) ancestors (Jews) today. Some of the radicalized Muslims also persecute Christians. As with all races and religions, there are both good and bad. I am friends with both Muslims and Jews, and I feel sad when these good people are put in the category of the radicals in their religion. Sadly, some professed Christians definitely do not act as Christians. Truth is, we are all God's children. As a Christian, I believe Christianity is the only religion with a Savior who died for our sins, was buried, arose on the third day, descended into Heaven and is ALIVE today. I believe Jesus has gone to prepare a place for all believers to have eternal life. This definitely causes me to want everyone to have the same belief and share the joy of everlasting life in Heaven. As much as I wish this could happen now, again we will have to "wait for the Lord".

Today realize some problems, such as health, relationships, your future, etc., are out of your complete control and cannot be solved quickly. You should pray for God's guidance. It is wise to keep preparing for whatever may come your way, but sometimes the best thing you can do is not obsess over the "what if's" and enjoy the "what now's". Just have faith everything will work out for the best and "wait on the Lord". He will lead you in the right direction.

....eXceeding great and precious promises are given to us. 2 Peter 1:4 (Grandmomma's Interpretation)

I am certainly tempted to use plagiarism for this verse. In this chapter Peter explains very clearly what I would like for you to know and believe. Peter even sounded like I do when he said, "Therefore, I will always remind you about these things—even though you already know them and are standing firm in the truth you have been taught. And it is only right that I should keep on reminding you as long as I live. For our Lord Jesus Christ has shown me that I must soon leave this earthly life, so I will work hard to make sure you always remember these things after I am gone." 2 Peter 1:12-15 (New Living Translation) Like Peter, I will continue to try to guide you to a Godly life for as long as I live. I do this for your sake because I love you so much and want you to escape the corruption in the world and receive the great promises of God. I plan on having many more years of giving my unsolicited advice.

Today read all of 2 Peter 1. Pay attention to the message. Take Peter's advice and add goodness, knowledge, self-control, perseverance, godliness, mutual affection and love to your life. That is a big order. Maybe you can pick just one to work on today. With these qualities in your life, you will not stumble and will receive the great and precious promises from God.

Yes, God is mighty, but He despises no one; He understands all things. Job 36:5 (Holman Christian Standard Bible)

I now know why you hear about the "patience of Job". This book contains too much to tell on one page. Job was a very wealthy man and was described by God as the most righteous man on earth. Satan felt Job was faithful because God protected him and he had no problems. Satan challenged God to test Job's faithfulness without God's protection. God agreed. The only restriction God gave Satan was Job's life was to be spared. Satan killed Job's family and removed his health and wealth so he would curse God. If anything could go wrong, it happened to Job. Through all his suffering, Job did not curse God. He did, however, question God. Three of his so-called friends told him he was suffering because of his sin, which was the commonly accepted belief at that time. Elihu, another friend, had remained silent out of respect for his elders. He could no longer remain silent and told all involved how they had been wrong. Elihu was younger, but God had given him understanding. This verse was part of Elihu's speech. He told them God will be there for all of us when we are at our lowest. God loves us and understands all things. We all are sinners. God wants us to be aware of our previous sins and be willing to learn from our mistakes. Elihu also showed us even the young can lead when God is their guide.

Today check out the story of Job. Some people may find it is easier to be faithful to God when all is going well. Others only seem to call on God when they are in need of His help. How do you react when things are bad? Do you have faith that God loves you and will help you, or do you tend to blame God for your problems? God sometimes uses our suffering to bring us closer to Him. I feel sometimes God doesn't change our situation because He is trying to change our hearts.

Zion stretches out her hands, but there is no one to comfort her. The LORD has decreed for Jacob that his neighbors become his foes; Jerusalem has become an unclean thing among them. Lamentations 1:17 (New International Version)

The people of Zion (Jerusalem) had become so evil and God was very displeased. He had had enough and felt they should be punished. He no longer helped them against their enemies and allowed them to be conquered and taken into exile. God did eventually forgive them and help them restore their great city, but never to its original splendor. God will always forgive us for our evil ways, but He will sometimes allow us to suffer the consequences of our sins.

Today think of the times you have done something you knew was wrong. Did you get caught? What were the consequences? If you did not get caught were you honestly proud or did you feel guilty? I certainly hope you did feel guilt. If not, you are too comfortable in doing what is wrong. This can lead to many bad decisions in the future. "Never do what you would undo if caught." Leah Arendt

Chapter Six

......As for me and my house, we will serve the LORD. Joshua 24:15 (New International Version)

Joshua spoke these words thousands of years ago after he had led God's chosen people into the Promised Land. Even though God had made it known through Moses that there should be no other gods before Him, many of His people did not follow this commandment. They worshiped "the gods their fathers served in the region beyond the River, or the gods of the Amorites in whose land they dwelled" (Joshua 12:15 NIV). Sadly, even today this is true. In some countries, such as India, the people literally have millions of gods. They worship everything. We may think there are not many gods in America; however, some people worship their possessions, their jobs, their pleasures or even their vices more than the Lord, our God. God wants us to be happy and has given us many blessings. I can promise you none of these blessings compare to God's love. I am so happy I can say along with Joshua, "As for me and my house, we will serve the LORD."

Today put God first in your life and do what is pleasing to Him. God does not use any magic power to make you put Him first. He has given each of us freedom to make our own choices. Many try to fill an emotional hole in their life with money and objects, but that never works. Money cannot buy happiness, even though it may give you some happy times. Nothing or no one can give you all you need to make you happy. What is the most important thing in your life? Will it supply all your needs? God will. We should put emphasis on the right things. Your Heavenly Father wants what is best for you and will always be there for you. He doesn't make you put Him first, but He certainly would love it. I promise you will love it too.

But those who trust in the LORD will find new strength. They will soar high on wings like eagles. They will run and not grow weary. They will walk and not faint. Isaiah 40:31 (New Living Translation)

Waiting is not easy. Life is full of times when waiting is necessary. It was fun waiting on the births of our children and grandchildren, but even that waiting can be stressful. We have spent so much time in waiting rooms because of medical problems and then had to wait to get all the results. You have no idea how much we have worried about you and your future, and we are still waiting to see what happens. We are watching you go through the ups and downs of life and want so much to be able to protect you and help you realize you can make it through anything. I know when I was your age that would not have comforted me. It is amazing how my strength has been renewed when I learned to put my worries in the hands of God, who has always been in control. Giving up control is not easy, but I have found so much comfort in knowing God will take care of everything in His own time and with His own plan for my life. I'll have to admit that I still have trouble waiting on His answer. I have learned sometimes He gives me the answer by encouraging me to do something about the problem myself, whether it is to seek help from someone or to just do something I feel encouraged (by God) to do.

Today "Wait for the Lord". You are still young, but you have already experienced so much that could not be solved quickly. Be aware that God was with you and will continue to be with you in every situation. Of course, God doesn't want us to just sit around until He does something. Make the best of your time and be ready when He calls. Also, God can always use your help in preparing for His results, such as studying, doing your job, trying to do what will keep you healthy, etc. Then relax. "Biblically, waiting is not just something we have to do until we get what we want. Waiting is part of the process of becoming what God wants us to be." – John Ortberg

Children, obey your parents in the Lord, for this is right. "Honor your father and mother"—which is the first commandment with a promise— "so that it may go well with you and that you may enjoy long life on the earth." Ephesians 6:1-3 (New International Version)

Why, you may ask? They don't honor and understand me. It may be you don't understand them. We as parents do make mistakes. We are not perfect, but most parents want to lead you in a way that you will be able to receive God's promise of enjoying a long life on earth. As parents, we know it is not what we do for our children but what we have taught them to do for themselves that will make them successful human beings. We also have learned if we want our children to be responsible, we should put some responsibilities on their shoulders. Believe me, this is not easy. I think each of you will admit you love for your parents to do for you what you know you should be doing for yourself, and you put off taking responsibility for as long as possible. Believe it or not, it is sometimes easier for the parents to do it themselves than to nag you to learn responsibility. You are blessed with parents who love doing for you, sometimes to a fault. You are also blessed with parents who love God and have shared that love with you. Some children are not as lucky.

Today make every effort to honor your parents by showing them respect, accepting more responsibility and following their wishes without complaining. Notice how much more enjoyable your day is if you make your parents happy. If you have a good attitude about this you may realize it wasn't as bad as you thought it would be. One minute of pleasing them may save many unhappy hours of friction. Plus, it is what God has asked you to do.

Do not be anxious about anything but in every situation, through prayer and supplication, with thanksgiving, present your requests to God; and the peace of God that transcends all understanding will guard your hearts and your minds in Christ Jesus. Philippians 4:6-7 (New International Version)

Wouldn't it be wonderful to never be anxious about anything? Life will always have uncertain or difficult times causing anxiety. Medical research has also found many physical reasons for anxiety, and medicine is sometimes necessary. Medicine may solve your mental condition, but you will never have the "peace that transcends all understanding" until you give your life to Jesus Christ. Our greatest blessing and privilege is to be able to pray in every situation in our lives. We are to humbly and earnestly give our requests to God and to always give Him thanks for our blessings. I find, even though I am aware of God's presence at all times, it is when I seriously stop to really talk to God that I feel a peace which seems too good to be true. I often slip back into the anxious feelings, but God doesn't put a limit on our prayers. I will have to admit there are times when I feel as Mother Teresa did when she said, "I know God will not give me anything I can't handle. I just wish that He didn't trust me so much."

Today get on your knees and pray. Yes, you can pray anywhere at any time. There is just something about being on your knees that feels like an intimate conversation with God. I need to do this more often. When you pray be honest and know no request, concern or sin is too small or too large for God. He understands and is always ready to help, comfort and forgive. Your answer may not come as quickly as you would like or even be the answer you want, but talking with God will help you handle your problem. While praying you may receive ideas from God on what you yourself can do. Sometimes you may feel encouraged to talk to another person who might understand. Always remember to thank God for His many blessings and for caring for you. Be still, listen and feel God's presence and "His peace which transcends all understanding". What a wonderful feeling!

"Everything they do is for show. On their arms they wear extra wide prayer boxes with Scripture verses inside, and they wear robes with extra-long tassels. Matthew 23:5 (New Living Translation)

Jesus was telling the crowds and His disciples that the teachers of the law and the Pharisees want you to do as they say, but you should be careful not to do what they do. They love being considered to be the best and are quick to make certain everyone thinks they are special. Jesus told His followers they did not have to follow all the many laws of the Pharisees to get to heaven. We only need to accept Jesus as God's Son and do what He has taught us because it is what we should do, not because it makes us look good in the eyes of others. Some people do good deeds and then brag about it and make certain everyone knows how "good" they are. If you need praise, just look at the smile on the face of the one you helped. "The true test of a man's character is what he does when no one is watching." — John Wooden

Today be aware of the times you do something just to make yourself look good. It is okay to be proud of your actions and appreciate praise. It is only wrong when you would not do it unless it made you appear special. People will never really appreciate what you do unless they see how much you care.

Finally, brothers, whatever is true, whatever is honorable, whatever is just, whatever is pure, whatever is lovely, whatever is commendable, if there is any excellence, if there is anything worthy of praise, think about these things. Philippians 4:8 (New International Version)

Is your cup half full or half empty? Do you see the best in everything or the worst? Paul was telling the Philippians to look for the good so they would not become part of the evil of the world. This is also good advice for today. When you watch the news, it is easy to become bitter. People love to gripe or protest. I just saw on the news someone had challenged everyone to disrespect the American flag, and it is sad how many have taken that challenge. A Navy Seal, who had fought for that flag, then came on to remind us what the flag represents. I wonder how many people paid attention to him. It is not just on the news. In our homes, it sometimes seems there is more criticism than compliments.

Today when you start to complain or criticize STOP. Then look for something good in that situation or in another situation to distract you from the bad. Think positive. Be an encourager. The world has enough critics already. Yes, we will have bad days; but mostly our days are what we choose to make of them. Our attitude is 90% of the way our day goes. How will you choose to live this day?

Read about attitude on the next page.

Attitude

The more I live, the more I realize the impact of attitude in my life. Attitude, to me, is more important than facts. It is more important than the past, than education, than money, than circumstances, than failures, than successes, than what others think or say or do. It is more important than appearance, giftedness or skill. It will make or break a company…a church…a home. The remarkable thing is we have a choice everyday regarding the attitude we will embrace for the day. We cannot change our past…. we cannot change the fact that people will act in a certain way. We cannot change the inevitable. The only thing we can do is play on the one string we have, and that is our attitude……. I am convinced that life is 10% what happens to me and 90% how I react to it. And so it is with you…. we are in charge of our attitudes.

Charles Swindoll

Go to the ant, you sluggard; consider her ways, and be wise. Proverbs 6:6 (New International Version)

My main goal when it comes to ants is to get rid of them, not try to be like them. What did Solomon mean? This is what I found on the Internet: The ants swarm in the woods and fields. They work day and night, storing their galleries with food, building mounds which compared to their size are three or four times larger than the Pyramids. In sickness, they nurse one another. In the winter, they feed on their supplies. They certainly do set a great example. Can you imagine how productive our lives would be if we were more like ants? We waste so much time being lazy; and if we were thrifty, we would rarely find ourselves in need. I have heard all my life that the idle mind is the devil's workshop. The devil does not want us to live as the ants. Then we would be able to accomplish too much and not have time to get into trouble.

Today be wise and learn from the ants. A song I sang to your parents and to you about an ant asked, "Just what made that little ole ant think he could move a rubber tree plant?" The answer was, "He had high hopes." The song went on to say that when you are feeling low instead of letting go, you should remember that ant…. "whoops there goes another rubber tree plant". If you watch ants you will see they don't give up easily. They are determined little creatures. Sometimes all it takes is high hopes and determination to get things done. Take the word "can't" out of your vocabulary. Instead sing your own song of the little engine that could, "I think I can, I think I can," and you will have a life of few regrets.

However, be careful, and watch yourselves closely so that you do not forget the things which you have seen with your own eyes. Don't let them fade from your memory as long as you live. Teach them to your children and grandchildren. Deuteronomy 4:9 (God's Word® Translation)

Moses wrote the Book of Deuteronomy soon before his death. All but three adult males of the original generation of the exodus had died. Moses was reminding the new generation of all the laws given them and also of all of God's many miracles their ancestors had experienced. I am so grateful Moses wrote the Book of Deuteronomy and the second generation did follow his word and pass this information to their children after them. Now it is our turn. It is such a shame, with all our privileges and the freedom of religion in America, so many people still do not know about God's love. These people are not all from underprivileged backgrounds. They just were never taken to a church or taught anything about God, even in their own homes. The vocal minority has spoken and we are no longer able to teach about God in our schools. That is why it is so important for us not to forget all the blessings God has given us and all the times He has been with us in all circumstances. We are to share this with others, especially our future generations. This doesn't mean we have to preach to everyone. We just need to show God's love in our lives. The best sermons are seen, not heard.

Today use God's name. Comment on how "God certainly has given us a beautiful day" to someone who needs to know about God. Make others know how important God is in your life and how He can be in theirs. Then show them by your actions, as well as your words. People will know you are a Christians not because you bear the name, but because you live the life.

I do not understand what I do. For what I want to do, I do not do, but what I do not want to do, I do. Romans 7:15 (New International Version)

What would life be like if there were no laws? Would we know right from wrong? What if God had never given Moses the Ten Commandments? Paul addressed this question in his letter to the Romans. I'll have to admit sometimes Paul is too smart for me to understand, but he did get me thinking. If it were not for rules and instructions telling me what I should do, I don't know if I would always make the right decision, or at least it would be easier to do what I wanted to do instead of what I should do. God began His instructions in the Garden of Eden when He told Adam and Eve they were not to eat from the Tree of Knowledge. Did they listen? No. Do I always listen? No. God could have made us do everything His way if He had chosen to do so. However, He gave us freedom to make our own choices. He did not want us to be His puppets, but wants us to make our own decision to follow Him. It is amazing how much easier life can be when we know our limits. We avoid so much distress by doing what we know is right, another reason to go to the Word of God often.

Today be aware of how many rules you break. How do you feel when you do something you know is wrong? Are you sorry you did it because you might get caught, or are you sorry you did it because you knew better? Also notice if you see something you know you should do but you choose to ignore. Right or wrong decisions are not always made according to a specific rule. If you have to sneak to do it, lie to cover it up, delete it to avoid it being seen, then probably you shouldn't be doing it. So often we just know what is right or wrong. I love the saying, "Follow your heart, but take your brain with you." Not a bad idea.

Jesus wept. John 11:35 (New International Version)

This is the shortest verse in the Bible. When I went to Sunday School as a child we were sometimes asked to quote a bible verse. We would all hope to be chosen first so we could quote this verse. As a child, I didn't realize just how important this short verse is. Jesus was at the tomb of His good friend Lazarus, whose sisters, Mary and Martha, and others were mourning Lazarus' death. Even though Jesus knew He would soon raise Lazarus from the grave, He felt deep compassion for those who were suffering. Jesus' reasons for letting Lazarus die were good and part of God's plan for Him, but He was very sad for the pain it was causing. Jesus knew raising Lazarus from the dead would actually cause the religious leaders to finally take action to put Him to death. Jesus always chose what would bring God the most glory, and sometimes, as in Lazarus' case, it required pain and grief. When I visualize Jesus' weeping at Lazarus' tomb I also feel the love and compassion He has for all of God's children, including you and me. I know He is sad when I am sad and even sometimes cries with me. I feel comfort in knowing Jesus sees the big picture and is with me through every trial of my life.

Today close your eyes and imagine Jesus with tears in His eyes. Do you feel his love? Yes, Jesus was a human being with human emotions. He cares for you and feels your pain. God sent Jesus to show us the way we should live and to comfort us in times of need. He will be there to help in every situation in your life, always giving God the glory.

Know that the LORD is God. It is he who made us, and we are his; we are his people, the sheep of his pasture. Psalm 100:3 (New International Version)

God made us and we are His sheep. Throughout the entire Bible sheep are mentioned more than any other animal. Jesus is known as the Lamb of God, the ultimate sacrifice for our sins. Sheep were and still are very important in the Middle East. The people understood when Jesus used the example of sheep in His parables. Shepherds love their sheep and develop a close, intimate relationship with them so the sheep will know their voice and trust them. They feed, protect, search for when they stray, discipline them, comfort them when they are hurt or afraid and the list goes on and on. This is the way the Lord loves and cares for His people. What an amazing feeling to be loved and cared for by the Greatest Shepherd Ever. Are you listening for His voice?

Today imagine yourself as a sheep. What kind of sheep do you feel you are? Do you follow your shepherd closely or do you tend to wonder off in another direction? How would you feel if you were the shepherd watching over you? Jesus did ask His disciples to feed His sheep. He wants us to do the same. He wants us to care for others and to lead them to know Him, not just by our words but also by our actions. Strive to be not only a good sheep, but also a good shepherd.

.... Lord, I do believe. Help my unbelief. Mark 9:24 (King James Bible)

A man, who had brought his son possessed with an evil spirit to be healed, told Jesus His disciples could not remove the spirit. Jesus was upset that the disciples did not believe enough to perform this exorcism. The father then asked Jesus, "If you can, will you please take pity and help him?" Jesus replied, "If I can? Everything is possible for one who believes." (Mark 9:23 NIV) This is when the father said what most of us would also say, "Lord, I do believe. Help my unbelief." Unbelieving is not my problem. My problem is believing enough and having enough faith to know everything is possible with God. Jesus didn't say everything is possible if you are a good Christian and do everything right. No, He said all you need to do is believe. As I write this I believe I am not able to make things right, but God is. He has answered so many of my prayers. He really has answered all of my prayers, but sometimes the answer was no. My problem is I know as the day goes on I will start to worry about life situations, forgetting God is in control and will handle everything. This is when I will say, 'Lord, help my disbelief.''

Today BELIEVE. Believe in God, but also believe in yourself. Know with God's help you can tackle anything. Don't be afraid to try new things. If you start to think "I can't", remember "Can't never did anything." With God, all things are possible. Who knows, you might even make 100 on your math test (if you help God by studying); or, as in my case, lose those extra pounds I gained while Poppa and I were on a cruise (if I use some willpower.) One thing I have learned for certain. Life does go on, whether you choose to take a chance and move on or stay behind missing many opportunities and always wondering what life would be like if you had believed. "It does not do well to dwell on dreams and forget to live, remember that." J.K. Rowling.

My dear brothers and sisters, take note of this: Everyone should be quick to listen, slow to speak, and slow to become angry, for man's anger does not bring about the righteous life that God desires. James 1:19 (New International Version)

God's word is wonderful. I know these words came from James, but we are told everything in the Bible is inspired by God. This morning I had a heavy heart about something I can't fix. I felt I needed to express my opinion and this would make everything right. Then I remembered all the Bible verses I have chosen about not expressing all your feelings and to only use kind words. I had to laugh and thank God when I saw what my verse was for today. God doesn't desire for me to stir up anger and frustration. He desires for me to listen and pray. I must again realize God is in charge. If He feels I have something I should say, it will happen. If not, my opinion will not change a thing. My opinion may not even be right (but I doubt it... lol)

Today listen first before speaking. Do not just listen, hear. Too often we don't really pay attention to what is being said because we are already thinking of what we want to say. Always think before you speak, and remember to say only words that will be pleasing to God and to those around you. As your Grandmomma has always told you and needs to remember herself, "Two wrongs do not make a right," and "If it bothers someone it's wrong." I have said this more years than I can remember, starting with my children (your parents). It was only today, April 25, 2015, someone questioned me. Yes, your Poppa. He was doing something that was bothering me and I gave him my wonderful quote. He said, "Well, that bothers me." I had to decide if it bothered me enough to be upset or if it bothered him more. He won. So much for a good rule. I still say if you are bothering someone STOP! Don't keep a dispute going. Life is too short to waste in disagreements. Live in such a way to make the world around you a better and more peaceful place. Be a blessing, not someone others wish to avoid.

Not as Cain, who was of the evil one and slew his brother. And for what reason did he slay him? Because his deeds were evil, and his brother's were righteous. 1 John 3:12 (New American Standard Bible)

Have you ever experienced sibling rivalry? Well, it is nothing new. Cain was so jealous of Abel he killed him. Poppa and I just saw the play "Joseph's Amazing Technicolor Coat". Talk about sibling rivalry." I cried tears of joy at the end of the play when Joseph hugged his brothers. Although they were evil to him, he loved them and forgave them. (Read the story of Joseph in Genesis 37). My sister probably wished she could have sold me. I don't think she even liked me most of our lives, but now we are close or at least she accepts me. It is wonderful having a sister to talk to about family and memories. Poppa misses being able to talk to his brother, and I miss my brother. Don't take your siblings for granted. I thought I would get some advice on this subject on the internet; but there was too much information and I gave up. What is so sad is there are so many sites on adult sibling rivalry. The verse before your verse today says: "This is the message you have heard from the beginning: We should love one another." We each have the choice to make. Everyone is different. Both of our children thought we loved the other more while they were young. We didn't. They were both different and we treated them as such. There was no way we could make them understand this. Now they have children and they love each the same, but I bet you don't think so. Do you want to spend your life trying to get even or be even, or do you want to learn to accept each sibling's personality and learn to live with him/her and love them as they are? Nothing says you have to be best friends, but you also don't have to be enemies.

Today ask yourself, "Do I even try to understand my brother or sister? Are they really that bad?" When you get older, family, get-togethers will be a lot more fun if you don't let these bad feelings fester for years. By the way, if you need help check out the internet. Best of all, remember God is better than any website and will help you to understand, accept and even forgive. Seek His guidance.

Only be strong and very courageous; be careful to do according to all the law which Moses My servant commanded you; do not turn from it to the right or to the left, so that you may have success wherever you go.... Joshua 1:7 (New American Standard Bible)

The Lord spoke these words to Joshua after Moses' death. He had chosen Joshua to lead His people into the Promised Land. God didn't just tell Joshua to "go on, I'll take care of you". He instructed Joshua to obey all the laws of Moses. Joshua was to meditate on them day and night so he would be careful to do everything written in them. Yes, God is always with us and will always take care of us no matter what. However, He does ask us to live according to His instructions. I have found so much comfort from God just by learning more about His Word and learning what He expects from me. It is still a continuous battle for me to turn my worries over to God, but I strive every day to "Let Go and Let God." God had given Moses, not only the Ten Commandments, but many other laws to help His people know what was a sin. However, the priests, Pharisees and scribes added many additional less meaningful laws without God's authority, and made it even harder to follow all the rules. They did this so the people would have to give more sacrifices, of which a portion went to the priests; and it also made the religious leaders feel more important. I am so thankful God sent Jesus to teach us how to live without constantly worrying about all the hundreds of laws. Yes, we still need to follow God's will, but Jesus was the ultimate sacrifice. All we really need to do is believe in Him as God's Son and our savior. Then we will joyfully do as God told Joshua, and not turn from His instructions, so that we may have success wherever we go.

Today let God into your life. Yes, He is with you wherever you go. Just don't ignore Him. Seek His guidance in all you do. Pretend He is a friend visiting you today. Make Him a part of all you do. Enjoy your day with the best friend ever. He's also a good listener. That is sometimes hard to find in a friend. What a privilege we have to take everything to God in prayer.

Pride goes before destruction, a haughty spirit before a fall. Proverbs 16:18 (New International Version)

It is good to be proud of your accomplishments and your appearance. I definitely think it is okay to be proud of your grandchildren. Pride can be a good motivator. It is when pride is so strong you let it control your life it becomes a problem. None of us like someone who is always letting us know how wonderful they are, but do we recognize extreme pride in ourselves? Some people even make others feel bad so they will feel superior. How many times have you become embarrassed and over-reacted to something because it hurt your pride? Poppa said his pride and anger have many times worked together to cause terrible results. He said someone could say something to him in private that he would accept; but if it was said in front of his family or friends, his pride would set in and he would do or say something he regretted. Sometimes we let our pride keep us from acting in a way we know we should, thus a haughty spirit before a fall. I truly believe God wants us to live a life of which we can be proud; but, most of all, we should live a life of which God will be proud. We do not need to strive to be better than others. The only person you should try to be better than is the person you were yesterday. We just need to strive to be the best we can be and give God, not ourselves, the glory.

Today be aware of how you feel about yourself. Do you worry that someone is better than you and take great pride when you are able to prove this is not so? Is that how you should measure your life? Do you like to show others how great you are? Truth is, if you are good people will recognize it without being told. Also, they will appreciate your gifts for what they are. A gift from God. Don't let pride destroy your relationship with others. Then you will have something of which to really be proud.

Quicken me, O LORD, for thy name's sake: for thy righteousness' sake bring my soul out of trouble. Psalm 143:11 (King James Bible)

The psalmist David was a man of God, but this did not keep him from severe trials. It is believed he wrote some of his psalms while hiding for his life in a cave. In this psalm David was pleading to God to save him, not for himself but for God's sake, so others would see how righteous God is. It is very easy in times of trials to focus on the need for relief, rather than to use the trial to get to know God better. Often, we ask, "Lord, why is this happening to me?", when we really should ask, "Lord, how can I get to know You better through this trial?" God doesn't promise us life without problems if we love Him, but He does promise to be with us as we face our trials. I know in my own life I have come to know my God and trust Him because of the trials in my life. Sometimes when everything is going well we tend to lose sight of God. It also doesn't always come natural to immediately turn to God in times of trouble. In fact, some turn against Him and blame Him. We must always be aware God is with us and wants us to trust Him in every phase of our lives. All we need to do is ask.

Today remember practice makes perfect. Every time something is wrong today seek God. Sometimes I even ask God to help me find something I've lost. Life is much easier and more peaceful when we seek God first. He will show us the way.

Remember the Sabbath day by keeping it holy. Six days you shall labor and do all your work, but the seventh day is a sabbath to the Lord your God. Exodus 20:8-10 (New International Version)

I love Sunday, the Lord's Day. As I write this devotion I have a good feeling inside, mainly because we just got back from church. I was blessed growing up with a mother who always took us to church. I'm afraid too many times I complained because I wanted to stay in bed or do something else. Now I thank God for those precious memories of my hometown church and the Christian faith which has sustained me throughout my life. The church we attend now is so different from our Methodist church in Clinton, Tennessee, but the same wonderful God is worshiped there. Sadly, both of these churches have one thing in common which is common in most churches today. Most of the congregation is from the older generations and new generations are not attending church. If this continues I am afraid the churches will not survive. Without churches, some people will never know about Jesus and the life He provides.... a life of peace and love. God commanded us to keep the Sabbath holy. We are to set this day aside to worship God and to also rest, just as He did on the seventh day after He created all things. Our God is such a wise God. Setting a day aside, not only to rest our bodies but also renew our minds, can make all the difference in our lives. It is true we can worship God without going to church. However, meeting with other Christians, hearing the wonderful words of God and singing the beautiful Christian songs renews our spirit for the next six days of the week and gives us strength for a more complete life. Even though Sunday is known as the Lord's Day, we are blessed it is not the only day God is with us. Let us not just worship Him on Sunday, but every day of our lives.

Today remember your last Sunday. What did you do? Did you think of God? Did you enjoy your family? Did you live that day in a way pleasing to God? If not, look forward to next Sunday and enjoy the Lord's Day in His presence.

Seek the Kingdom of God above all else, and live righteously, and he will give you everything you need. Matthew 6:33 (New Living Version)

Jesus spoke these words in His famous Sermon on the Mount. What are you seeking in your life? It is sad to me that so many people never really find happiness and contentment. They are certain all they need to be happy is a perfect family, a good job, lots of friends, a nice home, a beautiful car, a perfect body and the list goes on and on. I have also known people who seem to thrive on being unhappy. It is as if they are afraid to be happy. The truth is nothing is a guarantee for happiness. What good are all the luxuries of the world if you are not content within yourself? This scripture is hard to believe until you feel the peace which comes when you accept Jesus as your Savior. Jesus was telling His followers they should not worry about what they will eat or drink, or what they will wear. He said God knows our needs and will supply them. It is hard for me to explain, but I have seen over and over in my life when God has given me things I didn't even know to request. Most of all He has given me the peace I feel from knowing He is in control, although I will admit I still have to remind myself of this when I start to worry and think I need to handle it myself. It is also when I accepted Jesus into my life I realized no one else and nothing else is responsible for my happiness. I am the only person responsible, and God will help me put everything into its proper perspective. A lack of faith can bring unnecessary anxiety into your life. Always put God and His will first and He will supply everything you need, not want, and more.

Today be aware of what you are putting first in your life. Often we get upset over what is not that important and tend to not appreciate what we should. Make a conscious effort to seek God's guidance in everything you do today. Trust Him and know He will take care of you and show you the way to really live. Keep the faith and never give up. "What a caterpillar calls the end of the world, the Master calls a butterfly." – Richard Bach. Enjoy your flight through life, following your Master's plan.

There is a time for everything, and a season for every activity under the heavens. Ecclesiastes 3:1 (New International Version)

I really do miss the change of seasons we loved in Tennessee. Summer, winter, spring and fall each had a special beauty of its own. Seasons in Florida may not have such a beautiful change, but there is some change in the weather. No matter where you live, you will never be without change. Times change. People change. Think of all the electronics we have now we didn't have even when you were younger. Each of us changes every day in our attitudes and in our circumstances of life. The only thing that does not change is God. Solomon reminds us in Ecclesiastes 3 that there is a time and purpose for everything that happens in life. Life isn't always easy, and there are problems along the way beyond our control. We may have no control over the seasons in our life, but we can control how we accept each season. We can make the best of each event and each season of change and wait with patience for God's mysterious plan for our life. Change can be a good thing. We can learn so much and become stronger in our faith by how we handle the changes in our lives. Poppa and I are now in the winter season of our lives. We are so grateful for all our blessings, past and present, and very grateful that God is always in control.

Today read Ecclesiastes 3:1-8. Solomon gives so many examples of the seasons of our lives and choices we have. Think of the season you are in now. How is it different from five years ago? What do you look forward to in other seasons of your life? Enjoy today. You will never have it again. Tomorrow will change into another today which the Lord has made. Rejoice and be glad in it.

Unlike the culture around you, always dragging you down to its level of immaturity, God brings the best out of you, develops well-known maturity in you. Romans 12:2 (Grandmomma's Interpretation)

Even when Paul wrote this letter to the Romans over 2,000 years ago, the people were living according to the culture around them. Paul knew the culture is not always a good influence. I wonder what he would think of today's culture and all the influences we have all around us, especially on television. How many times have you accepted an action or opinion you knew was wrong only because "everyone's doing it"? Just in my lifetime I have seen so many ways of life against God's will become a common way of life. Family life is lacking stability. More babies are being born out of wedlock or even aborted before given the chance to live. Honesty is no longer taken for granted in the work place, government, relationships and life in general. In fact, the opposite is more prevalent. It seems everything is okay until you get caught. Paul is right even today. The way of culture will drag you down to its level of immaturity. Don't become so well-adjusted to your culture that you fit into it without even thinking. Instead, fix your attention on God. God brings the best out of you and develops well-formed maturity in you. Then the crowd will see your contentment and want to follow you.

Today be aware of actions you know are not really pleasing to God but have become normal actions for you because they are accepted by today's society. Each of the bible verses in this book set an example of how we should live. God's Word will never lead you in the wrong direction. That certainly cannot be said about the ways of the world.

...... Vengeance is mine; I will repay, saith the Lord. Romans 12:19 (New American Standard Bible)

Paul writes in Romans 12:17-19 (New American Standard Bible): "Never pay back evil for evil to anyone. Respect what is right in the sight of all men. If possible, so far as it depends on you, be at peace with all men. Never take your own revenge, beloved, but leave room for the wrath of God, for it is written, 'VENGEANCE IS MINE, I WILL REPAY,' says the Lord." This is really wonderful advice, but it is very hard advice to follow. It is a natural reaction to want to strike out at someone who has hurt you or those you love. God tells us this is wrong. In fact, God says we are to repay evil with good. He doesn't want us to waste a minute of our life being upset for something He will handle. We never really know what goes on in the mind of someone who does something wrong. God does. He will know if it is something best fixed through kindness or through harsh punishment. Therefore, we should let God handle it. God doesn't want you to stoop to the level of the one who is wrong. The best revenge is to be unlike the person who hurt you. Your revenge does not change the other person's heart. It only changes yours, and not for the better.

Today do not strike out at someone who upsets you or your family or friends. Pray for God to help you follow the advice of Paul. Watch the reaction of that person when you respond kindly to their abuse. I'll bet it will drive them crazy. (This may not be what God had in mind, but is my mean streak speaking). It will also make you proud to know you are in control of the situation and have handled it in a way pleasing to God. Well, God is in control, but you are following His directions. Remember, God will take care of the punishment, even if it is only making that person realize he was wrong. The truth is, there is no way we can control how others treat us, but we can control how we react. I need to work on that mean streak and realize I too am wrong for having that feeling.

We can make our plans, but the Lord determines our steps. Proverbs 16:9 (New International Version)

I have heard it said, "If you want to make God laugh, tell Him your plans." It is an incredible lesson some of us have to learn. I believe God does have a plan for us and we need to seek His will in our lives. He gives us passions to follow and the free will for trial and error. Sometimes we may feel God's encouragement to go in a different direction. God wants us to be available to follow opportunities He puts in place for us. These may not be in our original plan, but are to be used for God's purpose. It is great to have goals and dreams for what "we want to be when we grow up". Poppa and I still have goals. You are never too old for dreams. Just remember to always follow the examples God has given us through His Son, Jesus Christ. He loves you and His plans are always the best.

Today look into the future. Yes, most of you are too young to make a final decision on your life's vocation. However, you are never too young to be aware of your interests and start preparing by studying and getting experience in choices you may have. There is no "perfect" anything, so do not look for it. God does not reveal perfect choices. Too many people are never happy in their job, their marriage, their family, etc. because it is not the perfect situation of which they had dreamed. They are never able to accept the bad with the good. You will always be frustrated if you are expecting perfection. I do have one correction. There is one thing perfect.... God's love for you. Isn't it wonderful to know God loves you and wants to guide your steps throughout your life and be with you all the way? Let Him.

…..eXcept you repent, you shall all likewise perish. Luke 13:3 (King James Bible)

When the people asked Jesus about the death of some Galileans whose blood Pilate had mixed with their sacrifices, He reminded them of another tragedy when a falling tower had caused sudden death. Israel had rejected God's call for repentance, and Jesus was warning them not to think of the ones who died as greater sinners than all the others. He said these deaths should be a warning to all Israel to repent and do away with their false security of being special. A sin is a sin no matter how large or small. The same is true today. A sin is a sin and we should all repent and ask forgiveness for our sins, no matter how small or how large. Imagine you have a square box inside your stomach, and every time you do something you should not the box will turn. The more you sin (large or small) the more the box turns. Soon the sharp edges of that box are round and smooth from turning and cause no discomfort at all. The more we do what is wrong, the less guilty we feel until we have no guilt at all. Sins we ignore only become larger and eventually will cause problems for us or for others. We may not have a tower fall on us or have our blood mixed with animals' blood, but we will definitely be punished for our sins.

Today be aware of your actions. The word sin sounds awfully strong, but we all know wrong is wrong no matter what we call it. Confess to God and to yourself what you have done that you know is wrong and for which you are truly sorry. Even though Jesus said we should forgive those who sin against us seventy times seven and we know God will always forgive us if we are truly sorry, I think we all agree we should definitely strive not to repeat our sins.

"You must love the Lord your God with all your heart, all your soul, all your mind, and all your strength.' The second is equally important: 'Love your neighbor as yourself.' No other commandment is greater than these." Mark 12:30-31 (new Living Translation)

There were 613 commandments in the Torah (the law of God as revealed to Moses and recorded in the first five books of the Old Testament). The rabbis had many discussions about which commandments were of greater and lesser importance. When the Pharisee challenged Jesus by asking which commandment was the greatest, He said the first was "you must love the LORD your God with all your heart, all your soul, and all your strength." Deuteronomy 6:5 NIV) Secondly, "you should love your neighbor as yourself". (Leviticus 19:18 NIV). It is hard to even imagine a world when these commandments are followed by everyone. We have had wars, conflicts, family problems and so many other problems since the beginning of time. All of these problems would cease to exist if we all loved God and lived according to His will and if we treated others the way we wish to be treated.

Today remember these verses throughout the day. I know love is an emotion that cannot be commanded of us unless we are willing to accept the will of God and accept other's faults as we do our own. Try to put yourself in the place of the ones you find hard to love. Abraham Lincoln was a wise man when he said, "I don't like that man. I need to get to know him better." We should strive to love and accept others as much as our God loves and accepts us.

Zechariah said to the angel, "How can I be sure this will happen? I'm an old man now, and my wife is also well along in years." Luke 1:18 (New Living Translation)

Zachariah was a priest in the temple in Jerusalem and a very righteous and obedient man of God, yet he doubted the angel's words. Since we are given the "rest of the story" in the Bible, we can be certain Zechariah's doubts were wrong. Zechariah's wife, Elisabeth, did give birth to John the Baptist when she was "at a very old age". It is understandable he would have doubts. He and his wife were childless, and had prayed for a child throughout her child-bearing years. We may never have our prayers answered in such an important and miraculous way, but God never forgets our prayers. I have read many times of parents' prayers about their children being answered many years later. Just recently I read of a mother who had prayed that her grandchild, who was given up for adoption by her unwed daughter, would know Jesus. Through all the new technology, the grandmother had been able to find this now adult grandchild and see her prayer had been answered. It seems the child had been adopted and was the only one in his family who had been led by a friend to know Christ. Speaking of technology, Poppa has been trying all morning to get his computer to work, with no success. He just said, "Forget it. I'm going for a walk on the beach." Unlike the computer, God never stops working and we should never stop praying because His memory is never full. We may never see the answer to our prayer, but God's answer will be what is best and at the right time. We often learn a lot about life while waiting for the answer to our prayers. I feel God uses our time of trials and waiting to strengthen our faith and bring us closer to Him. I will always pray for each and every one of you, and I know that God will hear my prayers. I also will pray that you will be aware of His presence and His love for you.

Today do not forget to make prayer an important part of your life. In fact, strive to pray about every part of your life. Listen to God's guidance and never forget to pray for others. God always answers prayers.... yes, no or wait.

Chapter Seven

Anyone who belongs to God listens gladly to the words of God. But you don't listen because you don't belong to God. John 8:47 (New Living Translation)

Jesus was speaking to the Pharisees when they challenged His claim to have been sent by his father (God). It is a good question we should ask ourselves today. Do you belong to God? I remember the first time I really felt God speak to me. I did not hear Him with my ears, but I did feel His word in my heart. It was many years ago when your parents were still very young. I had awakened in the middle of the night because of so many worries on my heart. While I was reading the Bible, I felt such a peaceful feeling. I truly felt God was comforting me and giving me the strength I needed. I have always loved God, but I had never truly let myself "belong" to Him. The truth is my life has definitely not been all peaceful since that night, and it seemed as if I sinned more than I had before. I was told this is because I was more aware of God's desire for how I should live. Many years have passed since that night, and listening to God comes so much easier now. It may be because I have seen the times I tried to do everything on my own and the times I have asked for God's guidance. All I have seen has taught me to trust God for what I have yet to see. God has waited patiently for me to give my all to Him. He certainly does a much better job with my life than I ever could without Him. I continue to disappoint my God and myself, but He forgives me and loves me.

Today make a conscious effort to listen to the Holy Spirit within you. Be aware of God's presence with you through good times and bad times. Many of our troubles come from too much time on our hands and too little time on our knees. Give your life completely to God and you will definitely be in great hands.

But the LORD said to Samuel, "Do not consider his appearance or his height, for I have rejected him. The LORD does not look at the things people look at. People look at the outward appearance, but the LORD looks at the heart." 1 Samuel 16:7 (New International Version)

The chapter in which this verse is written tells the story of Samuel being instructed by God to find a replacement for King Saul. It is a very interesting story and one I think you would enjoy reading. Yes, God does look at the heart and not the appearance. We may have to work harder than God to see the heart, but no one will deny that a person's character is much more important than his appearance. That does not mean we should not strive to look our best. I feel appearance does show your character somewhat. I always told your parents that I didn't mind their messy rooms, but it usually meant they also had a messy attitude. There is a saying which has been around since the 3rd century BC stating, "Beauty is in the eye of the beholder." We each choose what we see as beautiful. Make your choice using God's example. Look at the heart.

Today be aware of how you judge others and also how you would judge yourself. What will others see when they meet you? Remember what my mother always said. "Pretty is as pretty does".

Come and see what God has done, his awesome deeds for mankind!
Psalm 66:5 New International Version

This psalm is the first of three verses concerning the praise of God. In this particular psalm, David gives a list of reasons to praise God. The fact that God is always at our side, always available to us through prayer, is certainly a great reason to praise Him. As I write this, I am in awe of something that happened to me this morning. Today I am scheduled for more testing to determine if the leaking of my aortic valve has increased. Every morning I have been reading a page from this book and then reading the complete chapter where the verse is located in the Bible. I have found it is I who needs this advice probably more than you. Anyway, this morning when I went to the page marked for today it was the one about the parable of the mustard seed. It was written on the day I was scheduled for the first time my cardiologist had ordered testing regarding the leaking of my aortic valve. So you won't have to look it up, I am printing that lesson (or whatever we call what I write) on the next page. This verse was the one I had planned to work on today. To me it was another one of God's miracles which reminded me again of how He has taken such good care of me…. so many times, I almost forgot to even mention I had a second melanoma removed yesterday. I feel God led me to the dermatologist to find these while still in the early stage. Miracles don't have to be of a biblical nature, such as the parting of the Red Sea. Each day is filled with God's little miracles to remind us of His love.

Today be aware of God's miracles. Just His miracles of the beauty of nature are all around us. Sometimes I feel God uses us to help in His miracles. Be aware of any opportunity you may have to make someone's day a little better. Maybe all they need is a smile.

(Don't forget to read my little miracle for this morning on the next page reminding me that God is definitely in control.)

(Read previous verse first.)

The kingdom of heaven is like a mustard seed, which a man took and planted in his field. Though it is the smallest of all seeds, yet when it grows, it is the largest of garden plants and becomes a tree, so that the birds come and perch in its branches." Matthew 13:31-32 (New International Version)

The Lord answered, "If you had faith even as small as a mustard seed, you could say to this mulberry tree, 'May you be uprooted and thrown into the sea," and it would obey you! Luke 17:6 (New Living Translation)

I chose these Bible verses because I have always loved the parable of the mustard seed and the examples Jesus used in His teachings. I will have to admit I am not sure if I could uproot a tree and throw it into the sea; although one time I did jump a wall and lift a lawnmower off Poppa. I know God gave me the strength because there was no way I could have done that on my own. Just this last week I saw a miracle I feel was an answer to faith in God. Test results showed my leaky aorta valve had progressed enough that serious open-heart surgery might be needed. When doing one more test to see what would be involved in the surgery, my wonderful cardiologist, Dr. Samantha Avery, found the leakage was not as bad as originally thought and surgery was no longer necessary. I know God did it, in spite of my doubt it would happen. I asked God for healing; but because He had answered so many of my prayers for health problems in our family before this latest episode, I really felt I was asking too much of Him. I did have faith God would take care of me, one way or another; but He showed me I needed to have more faith in my prayers. This book would be more than you would want to read if I wrote all the many times I have seen God's work in my life and in the life of others with faith the size of a mustard seed.

Today do not be afraid to ask God for miracles. He may not answer just exactly the way you may want, but His answer will come in His own time and will be the answer you need. Have patience and remember it does take time for the mustard seed to become a tree.

Do you like honey? Don't eat too much, or it will make you sick! Don't visit your neighbors too often, or you will wear out your welcome. Proverbs 25:16-17 (New Living Translation)

This verse tells me we should do all things in moderation. Of course, eating was the first example that came to my mind. We all have heard how we should eat in moderation. Some of you may need to play video games in moderation. Even exercise will cause problems if you exercise too much. Anything done to excess may be harmful. This morning I am seeing this verse in a much different way. There are many more ways we overdo things in our lives. It's hard to believe that you can overdo your love for God, but it seems I am tending to do that and may be wearing out my welcomed words. I have truly loved writing these what I am calling lessons for you, but what I am learning and feeling seems to be constantly on my mind. Too often, I feel I have the answer to everything in one of the Bible verses in the book. Yesterday I was so excited when I felt God had answered my prayers about a health problem, I felt I needed to share it with all of my friends. Today when reading Proverbs 25, God spoke to me through His word again in verse 20. "Singing cheerful songs to a person with a heavy heart is like taking someone's coat in cold weather or pouring vinegar in a wound." Many of my friends are suffering from bad health or other problems that are heavy on their hearts and I'm sure were not particularly comforted by my cheery "all you have to do is pray". They too have been praying, but sometimes our prayers aren't answered in the way we would choose. I don't pretend to understand why some prayers are answered and sometime God says, "No". I do know He has never told me "No" without staying with me and making me stronger.

Today notice what you may be doing to excess. Don't stop doing what you love, but be aware if you may be overdoing it. If you spend all your time and effort on just one thing, you might miss out on much more in life to enjoy. There is one thing I will never do in moderation. That is to love each of you to excess and beyond, just as God loves us all.

……..Elijah said to Elisha, "Tell me, what can I do for you before I am taken from you? "Let me inherit a double portion of your spirit," Elisha replied. 2 Kings 2:9 (New International Version)

The meaning of a double portion in the Bible is a double blessing. Elisha's request for a double portion of Elijah's spirit was because he wanted to be doubly blessed in his life and ministry. Interestingly, Scripture records exactly twice as many miracles through Elisha (28 miracles) as took place through Elijah (14 miracles). Elisha's ministry was one of the most influential in the Bible and continues to be remembered today. No, I definitely do not believe that Elisha was trying to one-up Elijah. He just admired his faith and his ministry so much, and he wanted to be able to continue his missions. I believe he felt he should not settle to do the same but should strive to do even more. There is nothing wrong in wanting to do better than someone else. That is, if you are doing it for the right reasons. Elisha did not ask to be twice as good so he could win an award for the best prophet. He wanted to be able to help more people and accomplish more on his mission for God. We too should strive to accomplish all we possibly can with any gift God has given us, always giving God the praise and Glory.

Today be aware if you are doing your best in whatever you need to do, whether it be school work, friendships, taking care of your health, chores at home or mainly using to the fullest all God has given you. "Always do your best. What you plant now, you will harvest later." (Og Mandingo). "Don't wait until you are too old to plant as much." (Grandmomma)

For I am the LORD your God who takes hold of your right hand and says to you, "Do not fear; I will help you." Isaiah 41:13 (New International Version)

Isaiah was a major prophet who spoke these words of God to the Jewish people when they refused to be faithful to God in worship. They were more accepting of the cultures around them than they were of God. What would you say to a rebellious group such as these people? God spoke through Isaiah, as only God would. It is easy to want to comfort and protect those who are in need and come to you for help, but God was reassuring His people that He was even there for the ones who had wronged Him. He wanted them to know he would always be with them, and they should not be afraid. God will do the same for us today. No matter how badly we mess up our lives, He loves us, forgives us and helps us get back on the right track. Even if you have placed God first in your life and are living a life pleasing to Him, there will still be times you will feel afraid. God knows your fears and will be there for you. All you need to do is be aware of His presence.

Today don't be ashamed to admit when you are afraid. This reminds me of a story about PaPaw (Poppa's dad). He was in an airplane during a really rough ride. Mamaw asked him if he was afraid. He answered, "No, but I am a little concerned." Whether you are afraid or just "a little concerned" always take a look at your right hand and know God is right there holding your hand and telling you everything will be okay. You are secure. Security is not the absence of danger but the presence of God no matter what the danger.

Give to the LORD, the glory due to his name; worship the LORD in the beauty of holiness. Psalm 29:2 (King James Bible)

I chose this verse because I thought it would be easy to memorize. As I usually do, I read it too fast and thought it was talking about the beauty of his nature. I felt you would be reminded of this verse every day, with all the beauty God has given us. When I read it today, really paying attention, the key words were to give God the glory due His name and His holiness. Then my mind went in a different direction. While writing this book I have noticed so many times I really feel I am getting ideas from God which I had never thought about before. Just yesterday I read an article written by someone who was at a ballgame and heard a Christian lady beside her say "Oh, my God!" when her child had made a mistake. The author said she cringed inside and wondered if this lady did not know that the Bible tells us not to use the Lord's name in vain. Truthfully, at that time I thought she may be overreacting, as I felt the mother didn't even think she was disrespecting God. When reading this verse, I had one of those "now I see" moments. We are to give God glory due His name. His name is God; and because it was so important to Him that His name not be used in vain, He included it in His special Ten Commandments to Moses. Like so many ways of life against God's will now being accepted by society, so are the slang expressions using the Lord's name in vain. God may know we love Him and mean no disrespect, but He did tell us very clearly that we should not use His name in vain.

Today when God's name slips from your mouth, be aware if you are giving God the glory due His name. Maybe even when you do use it in a way it should not be used, you will learn to stop and be aware of the glory His name deserves. Eventually, you may find it easier not to use His beautiful name expressing anger or surprise, but expressing your love and respect. Bless God's holy name. He blesses you every day.

He heals the brokenhearted, and bandages their wounds.
Psalm 147:3 (New Living Translation)

The book of Psalm is composed of 150 poems. They were written by a variety of authors, including David, Asaph, Solomon and Moses. The psalms are a collection of all the many different feelings of the people. Some are very joyful and full of inspiration, while others are very depressing or filled with anger. When realizing this, you may understand the Book of Psalm more and find comfort and joy it its word. Your verse for today certainly gives me comfort and reminds me I am not alone in my times of sadness. Just in the last week many events have happened that have taken me to my knees. Some I could have prevented by following God's instructions; but others, such as the accidental death of a precious young man, who was definitely a kind and loving man of God, was out of my control. Some wounds may take longer to heal than others, but God is always with us to help the healing. He doesn't care if the hurt was brought on by your disobedience or if it was out of your control. He loves you and will see you through whatever the situation, if you only trust Him and do not give in to your pain. Sometimes it may feel as if the pain will never leave. This is when you need to remember what your Nannie (my mother) told me...." Only time and faith will help." You may also find waiting for the answer to a prayer is often part of understanding the answer and will make you a stronger person because you survived another challenge of your faith.

Today, as always, if you are suffering any unhappiness go to God in prayer. Poppa and I certainly have felt the Lord carry us through our times of trouble. He will carry you also. Please read the story on the next page. Also remember to count the many blessings God has given you, not literally but in comparison to the hurt you are feeling. Who knows, maybe you can use one of your blessings to bless someone else in need. Sometimes the best way to help yourself is to find someone also hurting and help them.

Read the next page for more words of comfort.

Footprints in the Sand

Mary Stevenson, 1936

One night I dreamed I was walking along the beach with the Lord. Many scenes from my life flashed across the sky.

In each scene I noticed footprints in the sand. Sometimes there were two sets of footprints, other times there was one only.

This bothered me because I noticed that during the low periods of my life, when I was suffering from anguish, sorrow or defeat, I could see only one set of footprints, so I said to the Lord,

"You promised me Lord, that if I followed you, you would walk with me always. But I have noticed that during the most trying periods of my life there has only been one set of footprints in the sand. Why, when I needed you most, have you not been there for me?"

The Lord replied, "The years when you have seen only one set of footprints, my child, is when I carried you."

If your enemy is hungry, feed him; if he is thirsty, give him something to drink. In doing this, you will heap burning coals on his head." Romans 12:20 (New International Version)

We all know as a Christian we are to follow the first sentence, but heaping coals on their heads seems awfully harsh. What did Paul mean by this statement? When researching this term, I found Paul was quoting Solomon's words in Proverbs 25:21-22. So probably this was referring to an ancient practice almost 1000 years old when Paul used this term. I also found there are so many opinions about what this term means. As I think most of us tend to do, I read all I could find and then chose what I felt made the most sense. Of the many thoughts I read, I chose two that worked for me. You might want to do some research of your own to make your choice. It seems when this Proverb was written people heated their homes and cooked with fire. Sometimes their fire would go out and they had to go to a neighbor's house to get a coal to relight their fire. They would carry these coals in a clay stove upon their head. So, if someone were to give them a "heaping pile" this would be a very generous act. Just as a person really only needs one good coal to light a fire, it may take only one act of kindness to light the fire of the love of God in our enemy. Another common understanding is that by loving our enemies, we would cause them to feel the burning pain of shame and remorse, which would lead to a change in heart. In other words, kill them with kindness. Although that might work, and definitely would work better than being cruel to them, I believe we should be kind because it is the right thing to do, not just to make them feel bad.

Today discipline yourself to love your enemy. This is not an easy assignment. If you have no enemies you have certainly done something right and are definitely in the minority. It could also mean you have done nothing but sit around and do nothing to cause anyone to have an opinion of you, good or bad. Learning to live with people who disagree or dislike you is something we all need to do. You may never be able to impress someone who chooses to dislike you for whatever reason. Do not even waste your time trying. Just always do what you know is right and pleasing to God and enjoy life with your true friends.

Jesus told them, "This is the only work God wants from you: Believe in the one He has sent." John 6:29 (New Living Translation)

The word believe was written more than ninety times in the book of John. Reading Chapter 6 actually made me sad. In this chapter John tells of Jesus' feeding 5000 men, plus their wives and children, with five small barley loaves and two small fish. When evening came His disciples left in a boat without Him. They were frightened when they saw Him coming to them walking on water. The next morning the crowd could not find Jesus. They knew He had not left with the disciples, so they got in their boats and went to the other side looking for Him. When they found Him, they asked how he had gotten there. Jesus answered, "Very truly I tell you, you are looking for me, not because you saw the signs I performed but because you ate the loaves and had your fill." John 6:26 (New Living Translation) They asked what kind of work they should do for God. His answer is in your verse for today. "Believe in the one He sent." John 6:29 (New Living Translation) The reason for my sadness is because these people saw this miracle and some had seen many others, yet they still did not believe Jesus was sent by God and was the true Messiah. People today may not have been able to see the miracles in person, but we have the Bible to tell us even more than these people saw. Still the world is filled with those who do not believe in Jesus as God's Son.

Today do your share to help others believe. The Bible tells us Jesus rejoices more over one sinner who repents than over ninety-nine righteous people who do not need to repent. Jesus is already happy with the righteous as He knows they will spend eternity with Him in Heaven. Do all you can, not necessarily by preaching about Jesus but by living for Him. Strive to be more like Jesus and live in a way everyone will want to be like you. Let them see your love for Christ in your actions. Believe me, they will notice it; and some day you may be able to help them know Jesus as their Savior and live forever with you and Jesus in Heaven

........Keep a good conscience so that in the thing in which you are slandered, those who revile your good behavior in Christ may be put to shame. 1 Peter 3:16 (New American Standard 1977)

Have you ever had a guilty conscience, a feeling that something you have done is wrong? I have, and it is a terrible feeling. If you feel guilty and people talk about what you have done, they are probably saying what is true and you may deserve it. However, when you have a clear conscience and do what you believe is right, then the ones speaking badly about you will see they are wrong and should be ashamed. A perfect example is shown in the life of Tim Tebow. Tim was born to missionary parents in the Philippines. While pregnant with Tim, his mother developed dysentery and was given high dosages of drugs which damaged the baby. Her doctors recommend an abortion, but she refused. Thus, Tim Tebow was born. After a remarkable career in football at the University of Florida, Tim became a quarterback in the National Football League. However, his outspokenness about his faith in Christ caused vicious critics to ridicule his way of life and continue to search for ways to criticize him. The media seemed to favor the players with criminal tendencies and treated Tim's strong faith in Christ as a joke and were quick to criticize or make jokes about everything he did. The leaders of the NFL teams on which Tim played felt the publicity was harmful to the team's morale and would trade Tim. After many trades, Tim is no longer on an NFL football team. Tim Tebow is no longer playing the sport he loves, but is definitely serving the God he loves. He not only gives of his time, he also has a foundation which has helped so many.

Today notice if you are living a life you could defend against any criticism. Do not let any public or friends' influences or criticisms cause you to do something you know is wrong. Some people are always going to criticize others, especially the ones they envy. Let Jesus be your only role model. Then you will be able to hold your head high, causing your critics to "be ashamed when they see the good life you live because you belong to Christ."

Look straight ahead, and fix your eyes on what lies before you. Mark out a straight path for your feet; stay on the safe path. Proverbs 4:25-26 (New Living Translation)

There are many times when keeping your eyes on what lies ahead are very helpful. One of the first instructions given a runner in track and field events is to keep your eyes straight ahead because turning your head could break your stride and cost the race. I also remember your Grandpa Meredith (Poppa's Mother's father) telling me when we were planting a garden to put a pole at each end of the row we were planting and to keep my eyes straight on that pole or else the row would be crooked. My niece even taught me that if I look straight ahead while carrying a cup of coffee it would not spill. She was right. When I look down at the cup it is likely to spill, but looking straight ahead keeps it steady. Solomon was describing a much more important reason for keeping your eyes on what lies before you. In Proverbs 4 Solomon gives us the instructions his father, King David, gave him. David knew our hearts and minds receive feedback from our eyes. Wandering eyes are asking for trouble. You must establish your direction straight ahead and keep going to the single goal of pleasing the Lord. When we mark a straight path to Jesus and remember His teachings in every step we take, we will know we are on a very safe path.

Today check your vision. What do you see when you fix your eyes on what lies before you? Do you see new purchases for your pleasure or do you see the blessings you already have? Your eyes select objects and direct your movements toward them, but it is your heart and mind that give and receive feedback from your eyes. The Christian life is a race (Hebrew 12:1). To win, runners must look straight ahead without being distracted by other things. Life is not a sprint….it is a marathon. Please keep your eyes on the best award ever-- eternal life—and you cannot lose.

"Martha, Martha," the Lord answered, "You are worried and upset about many things, but few things are needed—or indeed only one. Mary has chosen what is better, and it will not be taken away from her." Luke 10:41-42 (New International Version)

I'm afraid I will have to admit this story has always troubled me. Jesus was visiting at the home of Martha and her sister, Mary. Martha was busying herself making things presentable for such a special guest and preparing food for Him, while her sister was sitting at Jesus' feet listening to His every word. Martha finally asked Jesus if he thought it was fair that Mary was just sitting there and not helping. His answer is in today's verse. When I think back of the many times years ago when we entertained more, I seldom really enjoyed my company for worrying about the house and everything else. These days I worry because I am not able to prepare for company as I once did, and I still get in a tizzy when someone is coming instead of being excited for the joy of being able to just see friends and family. One day when I was thinking about Jesus' second coming and imagining Him coming in a cloud outside our house, I probably should not admit this, but the first thing that came to mind was if I would have time to get dressed and put on some makeup. Luckily, I immediately thought "what does it matter". I get to see Jesus face to face. Yes, it is good to have preparations made, but nothing is as important as spending time with loved ones. Truth is, if I keep things in good shape every day, then I will be ready whenever we are blessed with company. The same is true with being prepared for Jesus and welcoming Him into my life. If I live everyday according to His will, I will be ready when He comes to take me home.

Today ask yourself if you are ready for a visit with Jesus. We have been promised He will return, "But about that day or hour no one knows, not even the angels in heaven, nor the Son, but only the Father." Mark 13:32 NIV. Some of us may have already gone to be with Jesus before He returns, but while we are on earth we should share His love to all. What a wonderful world it would be if we all were living for Jesus. Heaven has lots of room and the more the merrier.

"Neither this man nor his parents sinned," said Jesus, "but this happened so that the work of God might be displayed in his life." John 9:3 (New International Version)

Jesus gave this answer to His disciples when they asked the question about a man who was born blind. So many times, when people are faced with serious problems, they fear God is punishing them for something they have done. Sometimes others around them may have the same thoughts. It is true our bad habits and the way we live our lives may cause us to have problems with our health and life. However, Jesus made it clear that bad things do not happen to people because they have sinned. Some people become angry and blame God when there are tragedies in their lives. Others have faith that God will see them through and continue to give Him praise and show His love to all around them. The blind man about whom Jesus was speaking in this verse did the latter. I admire people who choose to shine even after all the storms they have been through. It is through their example I am reminded of God's love and compassion, and I find strength to make it through storms of my own.

Today read John 9. I am so glad I started reading the whole chapter and not just picking out one verse starting with the letter I needed. This is a beautiful story about how God used a blind man in His plan to show the world that Jesus is His Son and our Savior. Enjoy. The Bible is full of so many interesting stories. Follow the blind man's example. Trust God in all situations. Be able to say as this man did, "Once I was blind. Now I see."

One person gives freely, yet gains even more; another withholds unduly, but comes to poverty. Proverbs 11:24 (New International Version)

A story I read in my "Wisdom from the Bible" devotional book tells of two families who shared a home during the depression. The family living on the ground floor was always inviting others to share what they had. They were always willing to help whenever they saw a need. No matter how much they gave, they always seemed to still have enough. The upstairs family made fun of the way the downstairs family lived. They stored everything extra they had in a locker and gave nothing away. They felt quite content until they found rats had gotten into their pantry. Then they were very sorry for what they had done. Amazingly, the rats did not disturb the downstairs pantry. Selfishness can lead to so much unhappiness. True joy comes to us not from what we own, but from what we are able to give to others. Your Nan, my mother, had very little in material things but she was very rich in her faith in God and her love for others. She would give you the shirt off her back. In fact, she did just that. When she worked at the bank a lady came in on a cold day without a coat. Mother gave her sweater to her. She would always say, "It gives me joy." Because she gave so many her joy and was loved by anyone who knew her, even though it was snowing on the day of her funeral, the church was completely full. Mother was rich in the best way possible.

Today ask yourself if you are as generous as you feel is right. Do you find joy in sharing your material things and even your time with others? We all need to work on it. In my case, I am too selfish with my time. I will honestly say that I cannot remember a time when I was sorry for giving up what I call precious time to do something worthwhile. It just takes a conscious effort to do it. When we give what we have, God will bless us with more, and the blessings will be double because of the joy that giving brings.

Praise the God and Father of our Lord Jesus Christ. According to His great mercy, He has given us a new birth into a living hope through the resurrection of Jesus Christ from the dead. 1 Peter 1:3 (Holman Christian Standard Bible)

This morning was full of mixed emotions. Poppa and I have just returned from church services. Upon arrival at church we were told that our pastor and friend Dr. Mike Wetzel's father had died at 5:00 this morning. Dr. Mike was there to do his job of delivering the sermon. It was hard for him to do. However, he said when his father was band director, if anyone missed one performance he would give them an F. He knew his dad would be upset with him if he did not do his job. Also, as we entered the church we were given pink bracelets to wear in prayer for another faithful member of the church whose cancer had returned. Our pianist is fighting cancer but still shows up every Sunday playing beautiful music praising God. I had written about this verse before church, but it was just words. Now I am writing words I have seen in action. Dr. Mike, who is naturally mourning the loss of his father, was comforted with words spoken to him by his father's nurse. She assured him, what he already knew, that his father loved Jesus and there was no doubt of where he was going. Through all our sadness, we will always find comfort and joy in knowing even though we will lose much while we are still on earth, we will never lose our hope for a wonderful eternal life when we believe in Jesus. Of course, we always pray He will spare our loved ones who are suffering; but we know if that is not God's will, we all are promised everlasting life with our Lord and Savior.

Today examine your relationship with Jesus Christ. Do you put Him first in your life? Pray for everyone you know who is suffering; and when possible, share your love for Jesus with others so they too will be winners in Christ. Make certain you and everyone you know always remembers, "For God so loved the world, that he gave his only begotten Son, that whosoever believeth in him should not perish, but have everlasting life." John 3:16 (King James Bible)

Quick, Lord, answer me, for I have prayed. Psalm 141:1 (Grandmomma's Interpretation)

David was desperate when he prayed this prayer. He was literally fearful for his life and needed a quick answer. David didn't just decide to start praying because he was in danger. David had always been a man of prayer. Too often people forget to pray until they are in desperate need and then request a quick answer. God doesn't work that way. Not to say that God ignores your needs. He is more interested in your entire being. I would like to think I have always been a woman of prayer, but the truth is my prayer life has been a continuous learning journey. When I was a little girl I'm sure I knew to pray because I was raised in the church and Mother was a good Christian lady. However, I really don't remember doing a lot of praying. When my children were young I would say prayers with them at bedtime and tried to remember to do so at mealtime; but truthfully, that was more of a routine and being a good mother trying to teach my children about God. At the age of seventy-four, I now know that prayer is really a relationship with God and I sincerely count on God's guidance in all I do. I still disappoint Him too often, but He is always there to forgive me and lead me back on the right path. I have also found so many of my prayers have definitely not been answered quickly. In fact, I am still waiting on some answers. It has been said God answers in three ways.... yes, no, or wait. Whatever His answer has been, it has always been for my good and He has supplied all my needs and then some.

Today remember to pray. You don't have to stop and use fancy words. You can talk to God at any time and in any place. He is always ready to listen and loves when you listen to Him. Make prayer such a normal part of your life that you will quickly turn to God for guidance, comfort and don't forget thanksgiving.

"Remember the days of old; consider the generations long past. Ask your father and he will tell you, your elders, and they will explain to you". Deuteronomy 32:7 (New International Version)

At your age, it may not seem very important to know about your ancestors. It wasn't to me either. Now I would love to know about my family and there is no one alive to ask. The few memories I have are treasured memories. I remember very little about my "Granny", but I have sweet memories of her singing the beautiful hymn "In the Garden" as she worked around the house. The love for that song was passed to my mother, to me and now most of you know this song by memory. The main reason I started this book was to share my faith in God with you and help you understand the importance of the lessons which have been passed down to us in the Holy Bible. I want so much for you to feel "the peace of God, which surpasses all understanding." Philippians 4:7 (English Standard Version) I know I cannot just push a button or say a magic word to give you this peaceful feeling. I wish I could say I have always felt this peace. The truth is, I wasted so much of my life knowing about the promises of God and the examples Jesus demonstrated to us for the life we should live; but I only listened about it at church and then went on my way trying to handle things myself. I will not begin to claim that I do not fall back into my old tendencies to worry and doubt, but it is so much easier now to stop and seek God's help and comfort. I pray someday my words and hopefully some of my actions might plant the seed in your heart to give your life to Christ and trust Him to meet your every need.

Today ask yourself what you believe it means to really be a Christian. The Christian life is not a constant high. There will be moments of deep discouragement. This is when you need to be aware that Jesus did not leave you alone. His Holy Spirit is within you always for comfort and help. Accept this precious gift and find that special peace, knowing God will handled your needs. Sometimes you must remember God is always on His own time frame and knows what He is doing. Have faith and then pass it on.

So, whether you eat or drink, or whatever you do, do it all for the glory of God. 1 Corinthians 10:31 (New International Version)

Your Poppa has always been a very disciplined person. When he was getting ready to go to work you could almost set your clock by what he was doing, as he did the same thing in the same order every day. I, on the other hand, seldom do the same thing twice. I was able to write this book because of your Poppa's discipline. Every morning for years he has studied his Bible and worked on the summary and opinions he is writing for you. I decided to do the same and was able to stick to it because he was setting the time. It is true you can be a Christian without extreme discipline. However, making a special effort to have Christian habits is most helpful in living the life Christ desires. Whether we like to admit it or not, going to church every Sunday is a habit…a very good habit, but still a habit. If you miss a few Sundays it is easier to stay home. The Bible verse for today reminds me of a habit we should all strive to have. When your parents were little we would always say the blessing at mealtime. Then as they got older and our activities didn't allow us to always be able to sit down at our table for a meal, we would forget to thank God for our food. We were uncomfortable saying the blessing in a restaurant, and truthfully were usually in such a hurry we would just plain forget. I was also a more private person in sharing my religion at that time. I felt praying in public was wrong because of Jesus' saying we should pray in private. I now feel He meant not to make a big show just to impress others. Now when I see people quietly hold hands and bless their food, it gives me a feeling of appreciation and a reminder of God's Blessings.

Today make a special effort to thank God for everything you put into your mouth to eat or drink. A silent prayer is just fine. If you eat as often as I do, you will be praising God all day long. He certainly blesses us all day long. Thank Him.

This is the confidence we have in approaching God: that if we ask anything according to his will, he hears us, 1 John 5:14 (New International Version)

Are you a confident person? Is it easy for you to make a decision? The truth is, by not making a decision you have already made the choice to have no control over the situation. Have you ever thought of approaching God and asking for the confidence to do His will in any decision you make in your life? Try it. Do not give up the privilege of making the choices for your life. Sometimes I even to go to God for a simple decision or for help in doing simple things around the house. Just yesterday I was struggling just to plug in a lamp behind a large chest. I was so frustrated and finally just stopped and said, "Please, God, help me." It worked. When I told Poppa about it, he asked me if I really thought God had time to help me plug in a lamp. I thought about that and then realized God had left His Holy Spirit within me to hear my smallest needs. I had relaxed in my faith enough to just calm down and do it. No prayer is too small or too large for our God. Believe me, God has answered some really big prayers for me, especially letting your Poppa live through such terrible health problems. I know my life was saved by God's answers to Poppa's prayers and your prayers. Some of my prayers were answered very quickly, but it has taken years for me to see God's work in some of my hopes and prayers. Some He may have answered "no" or "wait. I definitely feel confident that God hears my every prayer and answers according to His will.

Today make the big decision in your life to be confident in approaching God with any and every request or problem you may have. God hears and will answer according to His will. Do not worry if His will is not the same as yours. Just know His will is always the best for you.

Understanding is a fountain of life to one who has it, But the discipline of fools is folly.
Proverbs 16:22 (New American Standard Bible)

When studying this verse today I read a story about a little girl who was warned by her parents to never go near the road. She didn't really understand why they were so strict about this, and one day she decided to get close to the road to learn why. While she was thinking about the road a neighbor's dog darted into the road in front of a speeding car. Even though the car tried to stop, the dog was hit and killed. She then understood what she had been told all her life. Many times we question things we have been told and don't see their importance. It is only when we understand the request and the logic of it that we are more than willing to follow the instructions. You will find the most important instructions for your life are found in God's Word. Our Heavenly Father gives us all the instructions and examples we will ever need. It is also wise to follow the advice of your parents and others who have learned from experience what you should avoid. When you refuse to follow these instructions, and have the discipline of fools, using lack of good sense, you are flirting with disaster. When you understand the importance of trusting God's Word and the warnings from those who love you, a long and happy life will be yours.

Today think of at least one time you did not follow instructions and wish you had. Surely you can think of one. If not, I promise you will eventually see the error of your ways. It is true, we do learn from our mistakes; but your life will have fewer mistakes if you avoid the folly (lack of good sense; foolishness) of fools and learn to trust and obey, even when you do not really understand the reason yet. "Life can only be understood backwards; but it must be lived forwards." Siren Kierkegaard.

…..Value others above yourselves, not looking to your own interests but each of you to the interests of the others. Philippians 2:3-4 (NIV)

When Jesus' twelve disciples argued about which of them was the greatest, Jesus said, "Anyone who wants to be first must be the very last, and the servant of all." Mark 9:35 (NIV). Putting others' interests before your own definitely does not come natural in today's culture. Today everything is competitive. From early childhood, pressure is put on everyone to be the best. It seems to be more natural to want to be better than others than to want to help them. There is nothing wrong in always doing your best; in fact, it is what you should strive to do. But the Bible teaches us to be humble and always do for others without thinking of ourselves. This is easier for some than it is for others. You can see a different attitude in the ones who are always aware of others' feelings and the ones who are just out for themselves. The self-centered people never really seem content and are always wanting even more or to do even better. The person who is always thinking of others first appears happy, content and is loved and respected by all. How do you feel when you know you have done something to make someone happy? The person you helped certainly thinks you are the best.

Today strive to think of others before yourself. While checking the computer for a quote to give you about helping others, I was really surprised to find hundreds of quotes written by very successful people. Each realized how blessed their life had been by being able to care about others. I couldn't choose just one of those quotes so I chose the refrain of a song that was sung at Mother's funeral because it described her life: "Others, Lord, yes others…Let this my motto be. Help me to live for others, that I may live like Thee." Let us all strive to follow her example and, more importantly, the example of our Lord and Savior, Jesus Christ.

We who are strong have an obligation to bear with the failings of the weak, and not to please ourselves. Romans 15:1 (ESV)

Everyone will probably agree the above verse is true. Some are stronger than others and should use their God-given gift to help those in need. When I read the story about the starfish on the next page, it made so much sense to me. I chose this verse so I would be able to use it in this book. As an example of the moral of this story, this morning Poppa got a call from someone we had known years ago. She was telling Poppa her husband had died and she was being evicted. Poppa was able to give her some legal advice, but we were still left with the helpless feeling of her situation. We know there are too many people in this same situation who need help. How do you know who to help and when? Poppa and I have always tried to help people whenever we could. We have sometimes learned afterwards that our help wasn't really needed and the money we gave them was used for something other than what we were told was needed. With the world now so full of people satisfied to live with handouts, it is easy to get discouraged about helping anyone. No, we may not be able to help everyone or to solve all their problems, but we should never quit trying. As always, we need to seek God's guidance and stay alert to the needs of others. We may make a few bad choices, but don't let those choices keep you from helping those who are really in need. Most of all, pray for the weak and needy. Sometimes that is all you can do, but sometime prayer is what they really need. (The lady who had called Poppa called back to say she and her son are in a new home and doing fine. Our prayers for this family were answered.)

Today notice the needs of those around you. It maybe they are only sad and need a friendly face. "No act of kindness, no matter how small, is ever wasted." Aesop

The Starfish Story

Adapted from the Star Thrower by Loren Eiseley (1907 - 1977)

Once upon a time, there was a wise man who used to go to the ocean to do his writing. He had a habit of walking on the beach before he began his work. One day, as he was walking along the shore, he looked down the beach and saw a human figure moving like a dancer. He smiled to himself at the thought of someone who would dance to the day, and so, he walked faster to catch up. As he got closer, he noticed that the figure was that of a young man, and what he was doing was not dancing at all. The young man was reaching down to the shore, picking up small objects, and throwing them into the ocean. He came closer still and called out "Good morning! May I ask what it is that you are doing?" The young man paused, looked up, and replied "Throwing starfish into the ocean."" I must ask, then, why are you throwing starfish into the ocean?" asked the somewhat startled wise man. To this, the young man replied, "The sun is up and the tide is going out. If I don't throw them in, they'll die." Upon hearing this, the wise man commented, "But, young man, do you not realize that there are miles and miles of beach and there are starfish all along every mile? You can't possibly make a difference!" At this, the young man bent down, picked up yet another starfish, and threw it into the ocean. As it met the water, he said, "It made a difference for that one."

Grandmomma's Note: Too often when I see so much needing to be done, I do nothing because I can't fix it all. Next time I'll think of that starfish so grateful to be thrown back into the ocean, remembering I can always "make a difference to one".

............eXercise profits little: but godliness is profitable to all things, having promise of the life that now is, and of that which is to come. 1 Timothy 4:8 (American King James Version)

Anyone who knows me knows I would love this Bible verse. It is no secret that I have never loved physical exercise. This verse is a perfect example of how you can find a single verse to prove just about anything you wish to prove in the Bible. The only problem is the verse is often taken out of context, and what you choose to believe is far from what the writer had in mind. Those of you who are active in sports realize the importance of being in good physical shape to be able to do your best. You do this by lots of practice. Even those of us who tend to exercise only when necessary will also admit how much better we feel when we are conscious of our physical well- being. Other versions of this verse state there is "some value in physical exercise". (I liked the one saying "profits little".) In this verse Paul was explaining to Timothy that although physical exercise has benefits for a little while, living a godly life will profit you forever. As repetition of physical exercise strengthens our bodies, we also need to strengthen our spiritual life by a disciplined routine of prayer and studying God's word. Our bodies may become frail and we may be physically unable to function, but God's love and comfort will remain forever when we study and live by God's Word and always turn to Him in prayer. We will also have the wonderful peace of mind, knowing because of our godliness we have the promise of spending eternity with Jesus in Paradise.

Today is the first day of the rest of your life. Begin this day striving to make the rest of your life the best it can be. You have heard me say, probably too many times, "Little by little big things are done." Start today making a special effort to study God's word and pray for His guidance to live a godly life. While you are praying, you might also want to ask for His help in giving you the desire and the strength to do enough physical exercise to live a healthy life while still on this earth. I certainly wish I had taken better care of my body when I was younger.

You feel hopeless because there's so much despair in the world. Remember that you are in the world and not of the world. The Holy Spirit within you can stir up hope if you will believe in the supreme power of God in spite of the wickedness of the world. Psalm 42:5 (English Standard Version)

What a beautiful verse. This was written by King David thousands of years ago, and is still true today. There is so much despair in the world and it is hard not to feel hopeless. Sometimes I feel the only hope we have is in believing in the sovereignty of God. This is presidential election year and some feel there is no hope in either of the candidates. I know God is in control, but I sure do wish I knew what He has in mind. One thing I do know is what He has in mind for my life. He wants me to trust Him and to live according to His will. I have no control over who will be President of the United States, but I still have hope and faith in my God and have control over how I choose to live my life. I read somewhere that we are suffering from backyard religion. We look out our windows and do not see past our own backyard. We think of only ourselves, our family and close friends. We need to also direct our prayers to our leaders, both nationally and in our own hometowns. We need to live our lives in harmony with our neighbors and set examples for others, especially the new generations. If there is ever going to be peace on earth it will have to start with each and every one us.

Today ask yourself if you are a peacemaker or a troublemaker. If your family was the world and you were the leader, what kind of world would it be? One of your Grandmomma's favorite songs gives wonderful advice. It says, "Let there be peace on earth, and let it begin with me. Let there be peace on earth. The peace that was meant to be. With God as our Father, brothers all are we. Let me walk with my brother in perfect harmony." We should all try to live by these words. Can you imagine how great our world would be if everyone lived in peace?

Zion hears and is glad, and the villages of Judah rejoice, because of your judgments, O LORD. Psalm 97:8 (English Standard Version)

This beautiful 97th Psalm begins with a great declaration, "The Lord reigns! Let the earth rejoice." I chose the 8th verse because it is my "Z". Please read the entire chapter to learn of the mighty power of our God. "Zion" is another name for Jerusalem, God's chosen city, and is surrounded by "villages of Judah". Zion was rejoicing in the Lord's judgments against the evil doers and the idol worshipers. God made it known throughout the land that He was in control and it was only He who was to be worshiped. Today, over two thousand years later, Christians everywhere are still rejoicing because God is in control. Yes, Z is the last letter in the alphabet. Everything seems to come to an end. The alphabet ends with a Z, and this verse ends the ABC bible verses with unsolicited advice I have written for you. There is one thing we can count on that will never end.... God's love for us. In fact, "God so loved the world that he gave his one and only Son, that whoever believes in him shall not perish but have eternal life" in heaven, the New Jerusalem (the New Zion, the final Z).

Today be aware of your blessings of another day. Life is like the alphabet. No day is the same, just as no letter is the same. Life on earth will someday have its Z or last day. Make the best of every day and live each day loving Jesus and inviting Him into your life. Enjoy the good days, because not all days will be good. On bad days, remember they will not last forever. We can make it through each day because God is in control. Yes, this is the day the Lord has made. Let us rejoice and be glad in it! Psalm 118:24 NIV.

Conclusion

It is now time to conclude this book. I don't know how long I have been working on it, but I do know I am going to miss "talking" to you every morning. Just since I started this book, each one of you has changed, with different interests, different problems and many new accomplishments. Poppa and I have missed being with you during all of this. We may not be with you in person, but you are always in our hearts and prayers. I hope these words of unsolicited advice may help you in some way. Just imagine how much advice you would receive if we lived in the same town. I really don't know how to pass on the peace that comes when you trust God to take care of you. Yes, there are still too many times I start to worry and try to solve everything myself. I soon realize I cannot, but God can. Life experiences and God's Word have taught be to keep the faith and trust God to direct my path and give me the strength to handle anything that comes my way. I pray you will find this peace also. Always be aware that God is there for you at any time for anything. Let Him help you. I don't think He would object to your calling on your old Grandmomma to help a little too. Call anytime. I love you so much!!!!!

My Prayer for You

When Poppa and I were in high school, we were very active in our youth group at church. It was called the Methodist Youth Fellowship or MYF. When your parents were in high school, we were the counselors of their MYF group. We made many friends and many happy memories during these times, which are still precious to us today. At the end of each meeting, we would form a circle, hold hands and say the MYF Benediction. This benediction is also known as The Priestly Blessing (Numbers 6:22-26), as this is how Moses instructed Aaron and his sons to bless the Israelites. I am going to close my eyes….no, I better keep them opened so I can type. But I am going to imagine we are all holding hands in a circle as I say this prayer for you.

May the Lord bless you and keep you.
May the Lord make his face to shine upon you
And be gracious unto you.
May the Lord lift up His countenance upon you
And give you peace. Amen

(Back-left) Gracie, Anna, Sarah, John and John Patrick Agee (Back Right) Chase, Darren, Logan and Trey Ridenour

(Front) Emma Bea and Lea Ellen Ridenour Agee, Roger Ridenour, Matthew Agee, Lyndall and Tina Ridenour

And they all lived happily ever after.
The End